T0309913

THE CLASSICAL MOMENT

Other Titles from James Schall from St. Augustine's Press

The Regensburg Lecture

Remembering Belloc

The Sum Total of Human Happiness

The Modern Age

The Praise of "Sons of Bitches":
On the Worship of God by Fallen Men

Docilitas: On Teaching and Being Taught

Marc D. Guerra, ed., *Jerusalem, Athens, & Rome:*
Essays in Honor of James V. Schall, S.J.

The Classical Moment

Selected Essays on Knowledge and Its Pleasures

James V. Schall

St. Augustine's Press
South Bend, Indiana

Manufactured in the United States of America

1 2 3 4 5 6   20 19 18 17 16 15 14

Library of Congress Cataloging in Publication Data
Schall, James V.
The classical moment:
selected essays on knowledge and its pleasures / by James V. Schall.
p. cm.
Includes index.
ISBN 978-1-58731-124-6 (hardbound: alk. paper)
1. Catholic Church and philosophy. 2. Christian philosophy.
3. Philosophy. 4. Knowledge, Theory of (Religion)
5. Christianity – Philosophy. 6. Essays. I. Title.
BX1795.P47S335 2012
814'.54 – dc23   2011039424

∞ The paper used in this publication meets the minimum requirements of the American National Standard for Information Sciences – Permanence of Paper for Printed Materials, ANSI Z39.48-1984.

ST. AUGUSTINE'S PRESS
www.staugustine.net

"We suppose ourselves to possess unqualified scientific knowledge of a thing, as opposed to knowing it in the accidental way in which the sophist knows, when we think that we know the cause on which the fact depends, as the cause of that fact and of no other, and, further, that the fact could not be other than it is."　　　　　　　　 – Aristotle, *Posterior Analytics*, 71b8–12.

"Sir, I love the acquaintance of young people; because in the first place, I don't like to think myself growing old. In the next place, young acquaintances must last longest, if they do last; and then, Sir, young men have more virtue than old men; they have more generous sentiments in every respect. I love the young dogs of this age: they have more wit and humour and knowledge of life than we had; but then the dogs are not so good scholars. Sir, in my early youth, I read very hard. It is a sad reflection, but a true one, that I knew almost as much at eighteen as I do not. My judgement, to be sure, was not so good; but I had all the facts. I remember very well, when I was at Oxford, an old gentleman said to me, 'Young man, ply your book diligently now, and acquire a stock of knowledge; for when years come upon you, you will find that poring upon books will be but an irksome task.'"
　　　　　　　　 – Samuel Johnson, Wednesday, July 20, 1763.

"I was glad when they said to me, 'Let us go to the House of the Lord!'"
　　　　　　　　 – Psalm 122:1

"When thou dost ask me blessing, I'll kneel down / And ask of thee forgiveness. / So we'll live, / and pray, and sing, and tell old tales, and laugh / at gilded butterflies, and hear poor rogues / Talk of court news; and we'll talk with them too / – Who loses and who wins – ; who's in and who's out – / And take upon's the mystery of things. . . ."
　　　　　　　　 – William Shakespeare, *King Lear*, IV, I, 10–16.

"We do not hold the common view that a man's highest good is to survive and simply continue to exist. His highest good is to become as virtuous as possible and to continue to exist in that way as long as life lasts."
　　　　　　　　 – Plato, *The Laws*, 707d.

"Whatever you read in the writings of men, and whatever you hear in all the speech of men, and whatever you notice in the eyes of men, of expression or reminiscence or desire, you will see nothing in any man's speech or writing or expression to match that which marks his hunger for home."
– Hilaire Belloc, *The Four Men*, November 1, 1902

Acknowledgments

The author wishes to thank the publishers of the following sources for the use of essays that appeared in their pages: University Bookman for permission to use Chapters 1, 17, 27, 27, 28: The Hoya at Georgetown University for Chapters 3, 7, 10, 13, 16, 44, 50; Crisis Magazine and Inside Catholic on-line for Chapters 2, 9, 11, 12, 15, 19, 20, 21, 24, 26, 29, 33, 35, 36, 38, 46, 47; Maritain Notebooks for Chapter 6; Gilbert Magazine for Chapters 4, 8, 23, 25, 37, 39, 43, 45, 48; Excelsior for Chapter 40 ; First Principles Journal on-line for Chapters 31, 52, 53; Saint Austin Review for Chapters 5, 18, 22, 32, 51; The Georgetown Academy for Chapter 50; Generally Speaking for Chapter 30.

Table of Contents

Preface

On October 20th, 1949, Methuen in London published a book of *Selected Essays* of G. K. Chesterton. In it is found a total of 61 essays. These particular essays were "chosen," as the title page says, by Dorothy Collins, Chesterton's long-time secretary. W. E. Williams's *A Book of English Essays*, which Penguin published in 1942, contains 64 essays, of which three are by Francis Bacon, seven by Joseph Addison, and six by Charles Lamb, all of whom stand at the origin of English language essays, as Montaigne does of the French essay. The 1959 *Selected Essays* of Belloc, which was edited by J. B. Morton and published by Penguin, lists 42 essays. Joseph Epstein's "Familiar Essays," entitled *The Middle of My Tether*, only collects 15 somewhat longer essays, while the Penguin 2003 *Selected Essays* of Samuel Johnson reproduces some 122 essays of this great man.

This Schall selection totals 53 essays. It is not a mystical number. I did not add 61, 64, 15, and 122 and divide by four to get 53. You actually get 66 ¾, not a helpful number page-wise. But still, 53 is a goodly number. It is not too long, but provides enough variety to catch the wonder of the essay form of letters. My earlier book, *Idylls and Rambles: Lighter Christian Essays*, has 54 essays. That number was chosen precisely because it corresponded with the 1949 Methuen collection of Belloc's *Selected Essays*. As I said then, and repeat here, Belloc is the best of essayists. His short essays in *Hills and the Sea*, *Places*, *Towns of Destiny* are simply magic.

The title of this book comes from the first essay, "The Classical Moment" – a moment originally recorded in a back yard in Cape Town, South Africa. The third essay makes a similar point, this time occasioned by the Welsh poet David Jones. The sub-title is also accurate. These essays, which, as is only just, conclude with Samuel Johnson on the very nature of things that end, are selected because, more or less, each in its own way touches on "Knowing and Its Pleasures."

I was indeed tempted to entitle the book "What Philosophers Play With," the title of the second from the last essay. And that too is a subject which runs through all these essays, the concern of philosophers about the *things that are*, about the things that fascinate and move us. One cannot, I suspect, be a philosopher at all without a "classic moment" in his experience, something with which, I am sure, neither Plato nor Augustine would have any hesitation in agreeing.

A book of selected essays is, I think, its own literary form. It is not like other books. This is its glory. There are, no doubt, long and short essays. There are sober essays, also what I call "lightsome" ones, and many that have a bit of both in them. I have no idea how many short essays I have written over the years, hundreds and hundreds for sure.

I love the short essay best, I think, because it allows one to write about just about anything. Belloc, in fact, has an essay entitled "On Everything." The intellect, as Aristotle said, is in fact "capable of knowing *all that is*." The essay is something of a proof of this insight. It does justice both to necessary and unnecessary things. Such is a dangerous freedom, no doubt. The essay is not, as such, exempt from the pursuit of truth, even if that truth exists in it in fantasy or humor or imagination.

Two previous books of mine, *Idylls and Rambles* and *Schall on Chesterton,* are likewise collections of the sort of short essay that I love to write. *The Praise of "Sons of Bitches"* and *Another Sort of Learning* are also collections of short essays. *Unexpected Meditations Late in the XXth Century* is what it says it is, though it is also more a collection of very short essays.

Over the years, I have usually had on-going columns in some journal or newspaper to write on a bi-weekly or monthly or quarterly basis. I have series that bear such titles as "Wit and Wisdom," "Sense and Nonsense," "Schall on Chesterton," "English Essays," "On Letters and Essays," and "Last Things." It is from these sources that most of these essays derive.

"Essay" in origin is a French word. As Josef Pieper said some place, the essay is looser than the "article" of Aquinas, which is a very tightly organized argument cut to the bare minimum to see the essence of the point at issue. Ultimately, the essay needs the article. The essay can speak the truth, no doubt. It has more the emphasis on what one holds as true, rather than on the strict logic of what is true. The essays in this book, however, tend to the latter category in spirit. We have too much opinion. Indeed, we have the opinion that only opinion is possible, a rather frightening thought. Opinion has its meaning and its place.

It is the conscious statement of what we think is probably true when we are not, and know we are not, absolutely sure of its evidence.

Socrates taught us not to be over-confident in what we know. But he also taught us that many things cannot be reasonably held, even when we want to hold them because we insist on living by them even if they are not true. Many essays in this book bear the words "reality, truth, mind, and know" in their titles. The essay is not an excuse for an unwarranted skepticism.

An essay is not an exercise in "thinking out loud." Rather it is thinking while writing, or even perhaps the writing is, in its own way, our thinking things out. Our audience comes after we finish the essay. We have no idea who this audience will be until it is out there. And even then few who read what we write about will let us know about it, though some will.

Chesterton's friend E. O. Bentley, in the Introduction to the *Selected Essays* mentioned earlier, said that Chesterton never liked anyone to read his own essays in his presence. Chesterton especially did not like to hear his essays to be read aloud, though they are often great when read aloud. I have tried it. Yes, the essay is to be read, I think, when the author is not present, or not even known, or, as in the case say of Johnson, long dead. The "Collected Essays" of the dead are often the treasures of our kind.

The essay is a noble art, I think. I have often been struck in writing an essay that, when we come to its last word, we know that it is the end of our effort. The words or phrases completing it somehow just seem to come to us, to state what it is we want to conclude in the light of the whole of the essay we have been writing.

A speech, it seems, once prepared, is given first in public to a definite audience that its hearers may later reflect on it in silence. An essay first appears in silence usually to be later read in silence. Yet, what happens in silence rises above the surface of the world when the reader responds to what is said with delight or doubt or annoyance or affirmation, when the reader speaks to another of what he has read in some essay that he chanced to come across.

These fifty-three essays are mostly written in the past decade. They are about things I have read or have thought about or seen. They appeared first in journals, student newspapers, and more recently in on-line forms. Ultimately, any essay hopes to be found along with other essays. In a collection of essays, however, the reader is not to be surprised that one essay will be on the size of the cosmos, while the one following it is on tragedy or pianos, or tyrants, or mathematics. Yet, such topics all belong to the same world.

In this collection, the reader will find talk of vice and sin, of reason and will, of beauty and transcendence. Many of my literary friends will be here – Charlie Brown, Belloc, Aristotle, Dante, Plato, Hazlett, Aquinas, and, of course, Chesterton.

A collection of essays, in the end, can be read all at once or one essay at a time. A reader can begin at the back and work forward, or in the middle and work both ways. Yet, in this book, there is an intuitive order that begins with our experience of precisely "The Classical Moment," passes through Beatrice and Baring's Eton, and ends with "What Philosophers Play With," and "Everlasting Futurity." A book of essays is a special kind of literature, making its own demands on the reader. These are usually, it is hoped, pleasant demands to be found here.

A wise tradition suggests that every man is, in some sense, a philosopher, not a professional one, to be sure, but one who knows when the *things that are*, as such, are truly spoken of. And it is one of the especial premises of this collection that each of us, writer and reader, also belongs to reality, to *what is*. We all seek, in our "classical moment," to be moved by the truth of things. In our lives and in our essays, in our reading and in our conversation, we have all been, to use Maritain's phrase in the second from the last essay, "touched by fire."

Yet, this is not a solemn book. It is in fact one that holds that the highest things are also found, most often found, in laughter and delight. There are reasons to philosophize and things we do not know. In the end, all is gift and we are moved by it. With this, we can begin these fifty-three selected essays at the "Classical Moment."

Chapter 1

The Classic Moment

Not too long ago, I wandered into Barnes & Noble on "M" Street in Georgetown intending to purchase the then new *Compendium of Catholic Social Doctrine*. They did not have it. To save money, if that is the purpose of life, I should have left at that moment. On the new releases shelf, however, for only eleven dollars, was J. M. Coetzee's *Disgrace*, a novel I had heard of and vaguely wanted to read. Thinking I could get it later, I proceeded to the upper floors where I found John Paul II's second from last book, *Memory and Identity*, which I did purchase, a remarkable book.

But in the process of looking, I came across Coetzee's *Stranger Shores: Literary Essays*. Though I am generally a "sucker" for these sorts of books, what immediately prompted me to buy it was the first essay in the collection, "What Is a Classic: A Lecture." I will have to maintain that a lecture can become an essay when written down. In any case, the lecture was originally given in Graz, Austria, in 1991. I took the book home and read the essay right away.

Coetzee's own South African background serves to provide the framework for this consideration on the famous question about the nature and character of a "classic," be it in literature, music, or even games. Coetzee, now at the University of Chicago, begins his considerations by recalling T. S. Eliot's famous essay, "What Is a Classic," a lecture given to the Virgil Society in London in October, 1944. Coetzee notes that Eliot barely mentioned the war in his lecture, as if to say, as C.S. Lewis said in his famous essay "Learning in War Time," that there are more important things than wars, even during wars, the chief of which are precisely classics, that is, reflections on beauty, truth, and *what is*. Without these, no one can know what he is fighting for.

Coetzee's problem in this lecture/essay is to define what a classic is. He is not comfortable with the idea that a classic has no history. He points out that many "classics" are not recognized as classics until many decades or centuries after they are written. The burden of his lecture is to see if the history of a classic's becoming a classic might itself be a factor in discovering what a classic is. Coetzee is not a debunker, though he takes some pains to examine Eliot's own relation between his American background and his British and London literary and personal identity, wherein he (Eliot) could better associate himself with the great western classical tradition, particularly with Virgil.

But what interested me most about this essay was Coetzee's description of how he arrived at the problem of what is a classic in the first place. It seems that Coetzee was a boy of fifteen, living in the suburbs of Cape Town in 1955. He was, as are many boys of his age, "bored" out of his mind, as he tells us, "the main problem of existence in those days." Nothing much was going on. It was a Sunday afternoon (I think of Kris Kristofferson's "Sunday Morning Coming Down"). Young Coetzee had no reason that day to think that anything much would go on either.

However, suddenly, from the house next door, Coetzee tells us that he heard some music that he had never heard before. He was not at the time at all musically inclined, still the music suddenly made him alert. This is how he describes the moment: "As long as the music lasted, I was frozen. I dared not breathe. I was being spoken to by the music as music had never spoken to me before."[1] His neighbors seem to have been transient students. He never heard the piece again though he listened for it. The music was Bach's "Well-Tempered Clavier" played on a harpsichord, though he did not learn this title till later. "At the age of fifteen, I knew (it) only – in a somewhat suspicions and even hostile teenage manner – as 'classical music.'"

It was from this experience that Coetzee later investigated Bach as a "classic," only to find out that Bach was not especially recognized in his own time and when he was later appreciated it was often for reasons other than his music, romanticism or German nationalism. Yet, it seems that there was always a tradition among musicians of playing and re-playing Bach. Indeed, music seems to have this requirement built into its very core so that what is a classic is examined again and again down the ages.

Later in life, Coetzee examined himself often on this initial experience. Was he moved simply because that is what "classics" do to us if we read or hear them? Yet, all of us know people who listen to or read

---

1   J. M. Coetzee, *Strange Shores: Literary Essays* (New York: Penguin, 2002).

classics who are not moved by them at all. "About my response to Bach in 1955, I asked whether it was truly a response to some inherent quality in the music rather than a symbolic election on my part of European high culture as a way out of a social and historical dead end." Thus, our love of Bach could be a sort of snobbishness. In the end, Coetzee thinks that it really was the music. But the very history of classics, the critique of them even, is part of what makes them classics. "The interrogation of the classic, no matter how hostile, is part of the history of the classic, inevitable and even to be welcomed."[2]

Yet, what interested me most in Coetzee's essay/lecture was not so much his social science ruminations. It was the raw fact that a human being, even at fifteen – there are people who have fallen in love in every proper sense at more or less that age, I think of Dante – can see or hear something that simply changes his life and, perhaps, in changing his life, changes the world.

This "Back moment," as I now like to call it, reminds me of nothing so much as the memorable passage in *The Confessions* where, at nineteen, in an obscure also African city, Augustine chanced to read a dialogue of Cicero. Cicero was another man who knew about and wondered about "what is a classic?" On putting the essay down, the young Augustine burned in his heart and wanted to become a philosopher, even though Plato said that nineteen is too young to be one. Moments that change lives and the world are like these experiences of two young African gentlemen who read or hear something that they never heard of and are "frozen" by them.

In conclusion, there is one other young man whom I like to recall, a young man who, at a similar moment, did not listen. This is the Rich Young Man in the Gospels (Matthew 16: 19–22) about whom John Paul II, both in *Veritatis Splendor* and *Memory and Identity,* speaks with great earnestness. This young man wanted to know what he had to do to be perfect – a brave question indeed. He was told simply to keep the commandments. That he had no problem in doing. He is next told that if he really wanted to be perfect, he should go, sell what he has, give it to the poor, and follow the man discoursing with him. We are told the young man was "rich." At this defining moment in his life, unlike the men in Cape Town or in Tegaste, he rejected the call. He went away "sad." We never hear of him again. This too is a "classic" scene, not

2   Ibid., 16.

perhaps of what is truly noble, but of what we are, people who can be presented with the highest things and not hear them, not see them, not understand them, or, more likely, not choose them.

Coetzee tells us, somewhat condescendingly perhaps, that "'What Is a Classic?' was not one of Eliot's best pieces of criticism."[3] Yet, when I read Coetzee's essay/lecture from Graz, what most struck me about it was his depicting Thomas Stearns Eliot, lecturing in London while "bombs were falling," and complaining only that, under such unpleasant circumstances, it was difficult to get the books needed to prepare the said lecture. Somehow, I do think that that wartime moment was, in its own way, as riveting as Bach's clavichord. I do not mean that to lessen the impact of a Bach or a Cicero either on Coetzee or myself. I simply want to recall moments that, in a brief instant, define the highest things and our response to them.

Whenever I put down the book containing Augustine's desiring to be a philosopher, I know that moment changed the world. From now on, when I hear the "Well-Tempered Clavier," I shall think of this fifteen-year-old in Cape Town "frozen" outside of himself. Whenever I think of Eliot lecturing to the Virgil Society in London in 1944, not about the war raging about him, but about the classics, what they are, I shall know moments that are, yes, themselves "classic." In the end, I shall hope, unlike the Rich Young Man, that, having seen, heard, and been called to these things that take us to the heart of *what is*, I shall not go away sad.

3   Ibid., 2.

Chapter 2

The Reality of Things

One Saturday in July, I was at the Jesuit Community at Loyola-Marymount University in Los Angeles, where a number of my, yes, "old" classmates dwell. On one of the campus lawns that afternoon was a display of vintage classic automobiles – Packards, Daimlers, Stutzes, Delahayes, Lincoln, Duesenbergs, Cords, Cadillacs, Willises, Rolls-Royces, Pierce-Arrows. Some of these touring cars, cabriolets, phaetons, roadsters, sedans, and coupes were definitely works of art. As these automotive gems were in perfect condition, it was easy to admire the craftsmanship that went into their design. Several of these cars I had never seen or even heard of before. Ancient things can also be seen for the first time.

Looking for something to read, a bit later that same day, I found a copy of Irenaeus of Lyon's tractate on the *Teaching of the Apostles and their Proofs*, in a French translation. I have always liked Irenaeus. When his *Against Heresies* appears in the Breviary, I always learn something. I was particularly struck by the passage that goes as follows: "The truth leads to faith, for the faith is based on the reality of things." The CCEL translation of the same passage reads, "faith is produced by the truth; for faith rests on things that truly are."

Truth is based on the reality of things! Truth occurs when the mind conforms to a reality that it did not itself create. But here we have Irenaeus telling us rather that this same truth leads to faith. Evidently, if I understand Irenaeus's logic, both faith and truth are based on "the reality of things." "But why does truth lead to faith?" we might wonder. I suspect that the answer is because "the reality of things," in their full understanding, leaves us aware that we do not ourselves know all this reality about even the smallest of things. The very purpose of mind is to find answers, but also to know when it does not find them by its own efforts or powers.

Irenaeus goes on, in the same sentence, to complete his thought: "The truth leads to faith, because faith is founded on the reality of things, in order that we might believe in things such as they are. Believing in this way, we thus might always protect, in their regard, the firmness of our convictions about them." Our conviction can be undermined by doubt about *what is*. It is a brave thing to say of *what is* that it is.

"For, as that which concerns our salvation depends on faith, it is necessary to have the greatest care for the true sense of things." Salvation depends on faith. We do not directly reason to it or merit it. We must care for the "true sense of reality." Another translation of the same passage reads: "Since then faith is the perpetuation of our salvation, we must need bestow much pain on the maintenance thereof, in order that we may have a true comprehension of the things that are." This is what our lives are about, "that we may have a true comprehension of the things that are."

What might one conclude from these comments of Irenaeus? The very first thing is that faith and truth are concerned with the very same things, namely, "the truth of things," the "reality of things." We have a hunger for being, for *what is*. How do we explain this hunger? I think we cannot properly "explain" it. It is already in our being before we seek to articulate its dimensions. It is almost as if we are given an initial unsettlement as part of our very being, an unsettlement that will not let us alone. We want to know reality, what is not ourselves, but ourselves too.

But "faith," someone might object, is not "reality" oriented. Faith is "beyond reality." It is precisely this "beyond-ness" that Irenaeus is intent on denying. Faith is not "beyond" reality. It is essential to reality simply because we recognize that our own minds, themselves radically oriented to *what is*, are not divine.

Chapter 3

On Being Moved

The Anglo-Welsh poet and artist, David Jones (1895–1974), spoke on the B. B. C. Welsh Home Services on the 29th of October, 1954. His talk, entitled an "Autobiographical Talk," was reprinted in his *Epoch and Artist*. This book was given to me for Christmas. Just recently I began to look at it.

The following passage in Jones's autobiographical lecture particularly struck me: "The artist, no matter what sort or what his medium, must be *moved by the nature of whatever art he practises*. Otherwise he cannot move us by the images he wishes to call up, discover, show forth and represent under the appearance of this or that material, through the workings of this or that art." An artist's capacity to move us presupposes that within his own soul something not simply himself has previously moved him.

Our lives are filled with our activities, our doing of things. We usually define ourselves by what we do. We are doctors, lawyers, or Indian chiefs. Such a listing of our occupations indicates that we have the capacity to act in the world, to make changes both in ourselves (the virtues and vices) and in our surroundings, in our polities or in our gardens. We evidently exist in the world, in some sense, to change it, as if it needs further attention. The world bears signs of incompleteness without us. We are the rational creatures. We know what is not ourselves. Man is also *homo faber*, the carpenter, the maker.

Yet, I have entitled this essay not "On Moving Something," but rather "On *Being* Moved." Jones's observation implies that, at the origin of the habit of art is something that happens to us before we do anything artistic. To put it briefly: Before we can move, we must first *be* moved.

In the *Phaedrus*, we find an amusing scene in which Socrates is finally lured out of Athens to walk barefoot along a stream called the Ilisus. Socrates says to Phaedrus: "Forgive me, my friend, I am devoted to learning; landscapes and trees have nothing to teach me – only people in the city can do that. But you, I think, have found a potion to charm me into leaving…. You can lead me all over Attica or anywhere else you like simply by waving in front of me the leaves of a book containing a speech." A book can be a "potion" or a "charm." We should know this.

Whether landscapes and trees can teach us anything depends, no doubt, on what we think to be their origins. If we think they originate in chaos, chaos is what they have to teach us. People in conversation in cities can evidently teach us something. Even their writing may also entice us, as it did Socrates, though the meaning of writing, as he says in the same dialogue, is often difficult to pin down.

The art of writing is one step removed from the landscapes and trees, as it is from the conversations with people in the city. Leo Strauss once wrote a book called *Persecution and the Art of Writing*. Here, Strauss wrote:

> The works of the great writers of the past are very beautiful even from without. And yet their visible beauty is sheer ugliness, compared with the beauty of those hidden treasures which disclose themselves only after very long, never easy, but always pleasant work. This always difficult but always pleasant work is, I believe, what the philosophers had in mind when they recommended education.

Reading is a very difficult, though pleasant work. Its beauty is not always clear at first reading. This education, Strauss thought, consisted in the ability to "reconcile order which is not oppression with freedom which is not license."

An "order" which is not "oppression" indicates a reason according to which we can agree to act. And "freedom" without license means that we do not do merely what we will but what is right to do, something that we can and ought to know.

But to return to David Jones's comment, we are beings who are first "moved." This means, no doubt, that we are not self-sufficient beings. And that may be the best thing about us. It means that we are open to what is not ourselves.

The artist, to move us, has first himself to *be* moved. The beauty of a reading or a landscape or a stream is not always "clear" at first reading or sight. The pleasure of knowing is often only realized after much work, much reflection. It is almost as if, in the depths of things, a connection is found with *what is* itself. In the very fact that we can *be moved*, we find a hint of the everlastingness to which we somehow belong by virtue of what we are.

Chapter 4

Four Philosophies

How we live is usually a function in part of what we think the world looks like. But it is also a function of what we want it to look like so that we can live as we want. My brother-in-law, Jerome Vertin, had a copy of Rawley Meyers's *Daily Readings in Catholic Classics*, which I came across on a recent visit. For September 29, I found an entry entitled "Philosophies." It did not identify exactly where the citation was from. It was cited simply "G. K. Chesterton." It looks like *Everlasting Man*, but it could be from anywhere in Chesterton.

Chesterton begins by telling us that a "reasonable man," that is, a man with only his natural reason to work with, can come up with some four philosophies that might, on the surface, "explain life." For those who go in for this sort of thing, this intellectual exercise might be called "diversity." You have your way; I have mine. We do not make any effort to resolve which way of life might be true. Chesterton adds that these four possible views of life and embodied in the great religions or in what he called, amusingly, "the wide field of irreligion." Everyone recognizes that he must make an effort to explain the picture of the world that would justify the way he lives in it.

The first view is the atheist or materialist view of the world. All is material and finally is mechanical. Chesterton acknowledges that this view is possible, though not very "bright or breezy." It does fit many "facts" of existence. But it does not explain everything. It does not explain too many other things, like freedom or mind. If we like to think that what we do must be all right, we do well to embrace a materialist view that takes the burden of responsibility from us. We do what we do for the same reason mechanical things do what they do. We end up being rather insignificant.

The second view is that of the "normal man" who thinks that the world has a "design and therefore a designer." Yet, this natural man with his natural religion still thinks that the "Architect of the Universe" is "inscrutable" and "remote." The distance between man and God was so great that we had little to go on. This second view is "perfectly sane." It is indeed, Chesterton thought, "the ancient basis of the solid if somewhat stagnant sanity of Islam." This view also justifies whatever we want to justify. We think we exalt God by negating any order. Whatever is done, God could do in some mysterious other way. This other way included making wrong right, violence justice, what is justified one day to be unjustified the next. Chesterton called this view "sane," I think, because at least it acknowledged a "designer," though one who might approve of anything, a designer without a *Logos*.

The third view is that of the Buddhist or some types of metaphysicians. The burden of life is so bitter and sad that man would be better to "renounce all desire and all division." He wants to rejoin a spiritual unity from which he assumes that he separated himself. He never should have separated himself from the All into what is himself. For Chesterton, of course, this view is precisely the opposite of sanity and revelation which wants to separate the creature from God, to guarantee the transcendence of God and the reality of the individual person. The glory of God is precisely that He could create and sustain what is not Himself.

Finally, there is the man Chesterton calls the "mystic" or the "poet." He is really a "pagan." What is his view of the world? "It is a twilight world and we know not where it ends." Chesterton had much sympathy for the pagans. In a twilight world, they may not exactly have been waiting for light, but they knew they did not have it. They did not know what the world was about. Yet they did not in principle exclude the notion that it could be about something. The pagan did not have a reason why he could not accept the light, should it come.

We should not be surprised that Christianity first went from the Jews to the Gentiles who were most like the pagans. The atheist, the Buddhist, the Muslim remain considerably more difficult to deal with. If we look at the non-Christian world today, we can roughly divide it into four parts: the atheists, best represented by the Chinese, the Buddhists/ Hindus, the Muslims, and the remaining Pagans.

Not a few strains within what is left of Christianity drift uneasily to one or other of these four positions. The orthodox view – many are called, few chosen – is still commissioned to address these four philosophies. It is, as Chesterton implied, possible to discover a natural truth in each of the four philosophies. No philosophical position is all wrong. Each has a point that circles about a truth that the human mind can know by itself. The truth serves as a basis for a potential openness to a revelation that would ground the known truth in a higher order. Yet, as history shows, some philosophical views remain more closed than others.

Diversity is not for its own sake. It is not a good thing that these four philosophies "exist" with no effort to distinguish their truth from their error, as if the effort made no difference. What is to be frankly acknowledged is that each of these views is today backed by powerful political and coercive forces that are extremely careful not to let the essential elements of the Christian faith be known and freely presented. The most open societies today remain those that are still "pagan," mainly non-Muslim Africa, which is why most missionary activities can be concentrated there.

Chesterton had the remarkable capacity to see and identify ideas and where they led. He was also sympathetic. Like Aquinas he was willing and able to see a truth within a falsity. But he also understood that an idea that is not true will close us off from the fullness of reality to which we are oriented. Chesterton's work, in this sense, served the purpose of spelling out what ideas were and where they led.

Chesterton saw that the way we live was, in fact, grounded in the way we understood the world. But the way we understood the world was often itself grounded in the way we chose to live and a refusal to acknowledge the aberrations in our four philosophies of life. Thus, Chesterton did not list revelation as a "philosophy." Rather it was something in search of a philosophy that could acknowledge and comprehend what it was for the Word to be made flesh. This is why it is not surprising, as Benedict XVI said in the Regensburg Lecture, that Paul turned to Macedonia, where it was possible to understand what *Logos* might mean and to a people who were open to the notion that the world might just have an "end." It is from this philosophy that it is possible to direct revelation to the other three of the four philosophies.

Chapter 5

On Saving Sinners

"If one knew, he wondered, the facts, would one have to feel pity even for the planets? if one reached what they called the heart of the matter?"
— Graham Greene, *The Heart of the Matter*, 1948, p. 124.

Plots of novels follow theses and enigmas found in theology. Even though we are all sinners, the question arises: "Is everyone, in the end, saved no matter what he does or thinks?" This issue arises indirectly from the famous position of Origen, somewhat revised in the works of Hans Urs von Balthasar, that, in the end, God will see to it that no one is lost. Stated in the form of a novel, the issue could be developed in many ways, in different eras and settings. One way might be that of Hamlet in which the sinner is deliberately killed in act of adultery so that his damnation, by common theological standards, could be assured as the most satisfying sort of human revenge. But could or would God still "save" him, even then?

While at a nephew's this summer in California, I was looking in the bookshelves for something to read. There I came across a Penguin edition of Graham Greene's *The Heart of the Matter*, which I had not read before. After I finished it, I kept calling it, in my mind, *The End of the Affair*, the title of a later of Greene's novels. In a vivid sense, however, the plot of *The Heart of the Matter* is about the "end of an affair." It is about whether God can "save" us even in the direst sins, deliberately chosen.

The lady involved in an "affair" with Henry Scobie, a British colonial police officer in a dingy west African country during World War II, finishes the book conversing with the missionary priest, Father Rank. Henry has just committed suicide, the most unforgivable of sins. His justification for so doing was that he claimed to have loved two women, his wife and his mistress. He did not want to "hurt" either of them, a sin closer perhaps to vanity than pride.

His death, as it turns out, however, was not "natural" but contrived.

Though he sought to make it look convincing, actually it was due to an overdose of pills. We are thus left with the classic plot: "Can God save even such a sinner, such a suicide?" Our sympathy and pity are certainly in Scobie's favor. We see ourselves in him.

Henry Scobie thought that the ending to his dilemma is a "deed" in which no one but himself would be "hurt." This act was, in fact, viewed fi y by his mistress, Helen Rolt, simply as a "mess." At this point, the priest, who had earlier and rightly refused Scobie absolution because of the reservations of his repentance, tells Helen that even though Scobie was wrong in his suicide, he thought that Scobie "really loved God." (272).

To this startling observation, Helen replied that "he certainly loved no one else." That is, in her view, Scobie really loved neither his wife nor her. To this position, in the book's final passage, the priest observes that she might be right there also. That is, logically, the stated reason for Henry's suicide was not valid. We end up with a God who "sees" what is behind our sins. The implication is that indeed Henry Scobie, in spite of his doing away with himself, is saved, or at least we can suspect so.

Earlier in the novel a discussion about despair is found. This is the great sin. The suicide is usually considered to be the result of despair, of not finding anything worth living for. Chesterton called suicide the worst of sins because it was a rejection of the whole world, of life itself. Socrates said that our lives are in the hands of the gods, not our own. "Despair is the price one pays for setting oneself an impossible aim," we read. "It is… the unforgivable sin but it is a sin that the corrupt or evil man never practices. He always has hope. He never reaches the freezing point of knowing absolute failure. Only the man of goodwill carries always in his heart the capacity for damnation" (60).

If we apply this thesis, itself a reversal of values, to Scobie, his justification for his suicide is an "impossible aim." He loves two women, itself impossible in its consequences. An evil man would not have any problem here. Thus, by implication, Scobie was not an evil man. So Scobie is indeed capable of "damnation" precisely because he has "goodwill." Scobie does not want to "hurt" anyone, but ends up, by his goodwill action, hurting everyone, including himself and those he says he loves.

In the novel, a young man by the name of Pemberton, a man of good family, also commits suicide. Scobie is sent out to investigate his death. "He thought of Pemberton. What an absurd thing to expect happiness in a world so full of misery.... Point me out the happy man and I will point you out either extreme egotism, evil – or else an absolute ignorance" (123). We have to be redeemed in our unhappiness. We cannot wait till we are perfect. Perfection won't happen in this life.

The reason Scobie liked being in such a terrible African place was that one saw people there as they really are. No paradise is near. Only sins and evils are found. Even God loves us in our worst. If He didn't, He could not love us at all for we are generally in a wretched and sinful state. Scobie is like those he sees.

While "praying" over his contemplated suicide, Scobie tells us his reasoning: "O God, I am the only guilty one because I've known the answers all the time. I've preferred to give you pain rather than give pain to Helen or my wife because I can't observe your suffering. I can only imagine it. But there are limits to what I can do to you – or them. I can't desert either of them while I'm alive, but I can die and remove myself from their blood stream. They are ill with me and I can cure them" (258). The "cure" is his self-inflicted death, the great sin of despair.

Henry Scobie no doubt makes up the rules. His rules go against what the Church teaches, the rules his wife stood for. The priest thinks that Scobie loved only God. His mistress was rather sure that he loved only himself. He loved Africa because there it was easy to see that if God loved us, He had to do so as sinners. What about hating the sin and loving the sinner? The novel does not romanticize suicide. It is a last resort that does not really "work" for its intended purpose. The hypothesis of the book is that it is possible to love two people all one's life at the same time. The facts in the narration, as it is carried out, embrace this conclusion. Henry does not really know what love is. Real love, to be what it is, follows the rules.

This book begins with a citation in French from the poet Charles Péguy. It reads: "Le pécheur est au cœur même de chrétienté.... Nul n'est aussi compétent que le pécheur en matière de chrétienté. Nul, si ce n'est le saint." ("The sinner is at the very heart of Christianity ... no one is so competent as the sinner in the subject matter of Christianitu. No one, if he is not a saint.") This is obviously the theme of this book, of the life of Henry Scobie. He is portrayed as the "holy sinner."

"The sinner is at the very heart of Christianity. No one is so competent as the sinner about the essential matter of Christianity; no one is so holy." Christ came to save us from our sins in our sins. The sinner knows the score, knows the need of himself "being saved." Sinners can be "holy" if, in their sins, they search for God, who is, first searching for them.

What sinners cannot do is make up the rules of reality, of *what is*. They cannot save themselves. And if they do make up the rules by which they live, they cannot guarantee that their rules will make those whom they sin against with their rules, happy in this life or the next.

Are we all then Henry Scobies making up our own rules that do not work? No doubt, to a considerable extent, we are. On the other hand, is there any consolation in the idea that whatever we do, God will save us? I find little. We cannot be saved by our rules. Explicitly or implicitly, there must be an acknowledgment of God's rules themselves designed for our real good.

Novelists pursue salvation in the midst of sin, for that is where most of us are, where salvation is most needed. Yet, as the tale of Henry Scobie shows us, when we reach the "end of the affair" and the "heart of the matter," "heaven remained rigidly on the other side of death" (36). Otherwise, all we have is this world.

"What an absurd thing it was to expect happiness in a world full of misery" (123). God loved Henry Scobie and Henry Scobie, in the end, may have loved God. But Scobie's way of loving God implies that he can "cure" those he claims to love. He says he can only "observe" God's suffering. The "heart of the matter" is that Henry Scobie did not know or accept the theology of the Cross. His ignorance may have "saved" him, but it saved no one else.

The priest said that Scobie "loved" God. His mistress said that he loved only himself. Christianity says that the love of God, neighbor, and self belong together. The sinner is only "holy" when he repents his sin. "Despair is the price one pays for setting oneself an impossible aim." This, not adultery, was Henry Scobie's real sin. With "goodwill" he did choose "damnation," thinking it was compassion for his dual loves.

Is then everybody saved? The "heart of the matter" is that this life is not the final location of our happiness. But it is the final location of whether, even in the miseries and particularities of our lives, we choose the conditions, the deeds, that will lead us to it. As the "second voice," in response to his prayer, tells Scobie in the Church, "I have been faithful to your for two thousand years.... The repentance is already there.... It's not repentance you lack, just a few simple actions..." (259).

What Graham Greene wanted to know was whether we could be saved even if we did not take the "few simple actions." Certainly we could be if we made up our own rules. The novel admits that making up our own rules will not make those we say that we love happy. Only those who have "goodwill" can be "damned." Scobie's eternity depended on his awareness of his own sophistry. Perhaps this is why, as the priest said, God could love him.

Chapter 6

The Reason We Philosophize

One charge against philosophy is that it is not "practical." Only if it is "useful" is it justified. This point was illustrated in classic philosophy by the Thracian maidens. They giggled at the two philosophers whom they saw walking down the road engaged in discussing elevated things. The two scholars do not notice the hole in the road into which they promptly tumble, much to the delight of the young ladies. What else would anyone expect of philosophers? Basically, they are useless.

A second, more ominous, charge against those who philosophize is that they are dangerous. The old accusers at his Trial said that Socrates made the weak arguments seem stronger, that he confused and deceived everyone with his worthless subtleties. Yves Simon warned the young philosopher not to give his soul to an unworthy, but charming, philosopher.

The main charge against those who do not philosophize, on the contrary, is that they are too busy to notice what is really important. About *what* is, they are "clueless." They never see the whole. They are so concentrated on consuming and fabricating things, mainly for money, that they have no time for contemplation, for knowing the *things that are*. The harshest word John Paul II ever used concerned someone guilty of "consumerism."

The mean between these extremes, as it were, is that we should both philosophize and still do practical things. *Deus Caritas Est* was also about this double responsibility. Indeed, the activity of "making" itself, our capacity for art and craft, involves a philosophical act of knowing what to make. One of the concerns of Sertillanges' famous book, *The Intellectual Life*, was to show how, for ordinary people, this combination of work-a-day necessity and philosophizing was possible.

The great definition of man given by Aquinas, through Aristotle, is that man is the one being in the universe that has both a mind and a hand. Without the mind, the hand is a claw. Without the hand, the mind is enclosed within itself, never to see the light of day. It sees only forms which have no concreteness. Still, the human brain, not private property, is the ultimate wealth. Without the mind, the real riches of the earth are not known or brought forth.

The human hand is the ultimate "tool" in the universe. Nothing but the voice speaks to others as much as the hand. The famous pleasantry that an Italian cannot "talk" with his hands tied behind his back has its truth for all of us. The robots that we see putting automobiles together on TV are themselves products of mind and hand. So is TV for that matter.

The reason we philosophize is because we want, whether we admit it or not, to know the truth of things. Socrates told us to begin this pursuit of truth by "knowing ourselves." Yet, we cannot even know ourselves without first knowing what is not ourselves. We have to have something not ourselves to activate our mind.

We suspect that knowing ourselves is a daunting, if not frightening enterprise. We know we are fallen. How far fallen we are not sure, but we have our suspicions. John Paul II was famous for telling us that we could not know the "whole truth about man" without Christ. "Was he just being pious?" we wonder.

We can well imagine the metaphysical perplexity of the Apostle Philip, in a famous incident in John's Gospel (14:7–14), when he asked Christ "to show him the Father." Christ obliges but chides him for having known Him for so long and still not knowing the Father. We can imagine the look on Philip's face on hearing this enigmatic response. Next Christ adds, speaking to Philip, that if he knew Christ, standing before him, he knew the Father. Philip had to figure it out. So do we.

One of the reasons we philosophize is that we come across such apparently impossible statements stated so matter-of-factly. On the surface, we have to conclude either that Christ is crazy or that some non-contradictory way exists whereby we can think our way through such enigmatic statements, whereby when we see Christ we see the Father. Surely, Christ knew Philip's IQ and that he had not read the yet unwritten *Summa Theologiae*, wherein he might have picked up a few useful distinctions.

Why do we philosophize? We can begin with two rather opposite premises. We can choose, whatever the evidence, to consider that the cosmos is bereft of any purpose within it. Nothing, we decide, indicates any intrinsic intelligibility in things, including in ourselves. This evaporation of meaning in things means that whatever our mind might be, however it got that way, it could not have been intended to be mind knowing *what is*.

Moreover, assuming that one has a philosophy that allows him outside of himself, this empty mind, when he uses his mind on the implicit chaos outside of itself, he alone gives meaning to things. He does not find any. All meaning is artistic. The human mind is thus the only source for meaning in the universe.

The second premise is that things have meaning, natures, forms. The mind, when it knows, is discovering what is already there. The mind does not make meaning but finds it already there. In this sense, philosophizing is initially contemplative. It gazes on *what is*, only to find there what is not itself, what it did not itself put there.

Why do we philosophize? We philosophize to explain why we can choose not to see what is in reality, including ourselves. Lucy is shown contentedly pulling a small wagon in which sits a stuffed dog. She is uncharacteristically humming a tune. She happily plays on the floor with blocks.

Then she hears her mother's voice: "Lucy, it's time to go to bed...." Next scene, Lucy jumps up and yells "NO!" Then she bends over, face to the floor, "I DON'T WANNA GO TO BED!"

Infuriated, she is up prancing through the room, "I won't!" Again, "I won't!" She adds defiantly, "You can't make me." Falling on the floor, she repeats, "you can't, you can't!" Then, crying on her back, she yells, "I WON'T GO TO BED!!! I won't! I won't."

Suddenly, she sits up half-dazed at herself. She says out loud, "Whew!" In the final scene, with blanket in hand, she is obediently walking to her bedroom, "Come to think of it, I AM kind of tired...." (*The Complete* Peanuts, February 23, 1954).

Why do we choose to defy what is good for us? Why is right discovered? Philosophizing must also account for the Fall, whatever it be called. Again, we can claim that there is no Fall. Whatever we do is right. But, like Lucy, why are we defiant against our own good? Why is it that we do not admit that our good is better conceived by another than by ourselves? Why is it that we are already *what we are* before we philosophize about what we are?

Advice to Thomists? "*Sola igitur intellectualis natura est propter se quaesita in universo, alia autem omnia propter ipsam.*" (CG, 3, 112).

Chapter 7

The Only Way You Can Be You

Recently, as my patient students know, Schall was sidelined with a bout of pneumonia. Relax, I am not going to tell you how well I suffer, because I don't, or the details, of which not even I have the faintest comprehension. But no one spends time in a hospital without some insight into his own uniqueness. Bottom line is that it is Schall in the hospital with pneumonia, no one else. You know perfectly well, however, that yours is not the first case of this infection that famously records its scourges, the one after World War I being perhaps the most notorious. My uncle Harvey died of it.

The other thing you learn is that you cannot do what you intended to do. Others generously come to your aid. Again the theme, Schall is finite. The fact of finiteness, mine and yours, is a thought to which I often return. It is one of the great metaphysical issues. Still, one has to be touched by students, faculty, fellow members of the Jesuit Community, and friends who want to know how you, in your finiteness, are doing. Each of these people is also a limited being in a world full of finite beings. The very world exists, I think, so that we finite beings, you and I, who come across each other in this time and this place, can know more than ourselves.

The fact is that sickness and pain have a purpose, both to indicate where the problem is and, in the Christian sense, to remind us to think of the redemptive purpose of suffering, itself the most enlightening of mysteries. Lent is in part designed to remind us of this connection, in case we forget.

The Holy Father in his recent encyclical, *Spes Salvi*, an extraordinary document, even encourages the old practice of "offering up" our suffering for the good and salvation of others. Why we human beings suffer brings us to the most profound mystery. We belong together even in suffering. Redemptive suffering is the path that the Father chose that Christ follow to redeem us. Suffering, even the suffering of the innocent, is not purposeless. Even our particular suffering or pain, which is so real to us, is modified by a walk through the very hospital ward you are in. There, you see others in far worse condition than you.

Yet, the real mystery of our lives is not so much our suffering but our wellness, our joy. Pain is easier to explain than delight. When one is sick, friends want to know how you are, meaning your health. When we are well, however, our bodies become secondary to what we do and know. Our bodies are the avenues through which we contact initially what is not ourselves, what is out there. But our sensory knowledge is directed to our minds, to figure out what it is all about.

Yves Simon has a remarkable passage in which he says that the only way that you can be you is that you *not* be anything or anyone else. At first this not being what is not you seems to make us isolated midst an abundance of otherness. The reason we are given minds, Simon adds, is precisely that what is not ourselves can become ours through knowledge. When we know someone or something else, what we know does not change what is known. This situation is something remarkable, really.

These powers of knowing and being, of course, suggest purpose. These things seem to fit together, our uniqueness and our capacity to know what is not ourselves without changing it. This is why the first act of our mind is contemplative. That is, it simply is amazed that something besides itself is out there, something that is not and cannot be ourselves.

Just after I made it out of the hospital, no mean feat, I received a card from a student in one of my classes. The card shows a collie dog running ahead by itself on what looks like an English country path. The path the collie is following winds off into the distance. Below this scene is found a passage from Tolkien. It reads: "All who wander are not lost." Wandering implies that we seek out, for no other reason than we want to know about it, what we do not yet know, what is not our unique selves.

The only way you can be you is if you are not something else. This is a profound principle. The principle applies to everyone. It is directly reflective of the richness of our existence as actual beings in the world. We are not the "immortals" but the "mortals," as the Greeks called us. We are the only ones in the universe who know that we will die.

But we are also the only ones who suspect that the death of our finite being is not our ultimate end. We have more poignant intimations of joy. Tolkien was right: "All who wander are not lost." Each existing thing that we wander into bears our condition. It could not be what it is unless it is not any of the other things *that are*. We are not lost. We are only wandering.

Chapter 8

The Basis of All Tragedy

The Defendant, the Newsletter of the Australian Chesterton Society (Spring 2004), reproduced a short essay of Chesterton "On Shakespeare." Though evidently published much earlier, it immediately comes from a book, *Chesterton on Shakespeare,* by Darwen Finlayson (London, 1971). At some point, apparently, Chesterton had intended, in addition to books on Chaucer, Dickens, Stevenson, and Browning, to publish a book on Shakespeare. He never got around to it, though he did write many essays and reviews on Shakespeare. I had never seen either this book or this essay before, but it has, I think, some profound things to say. Let me see if I can spell them out.

Naturally, Chesterton begins this essay with a comment on tragedy. We must be prepared for what he says as it is a jolt to us and our self-conceit if our lives are disordered. He tells us that all tragedy is built on one principle, the notion of "the continuity of human life." That is to say, like tragedy, our lives have, or will have, a beginning, a middle, and an end. Nothing is more certain. Our individual lives, whoever we are, constitute a continuum so that it is the same man or woman who does this or that deed in youth who does something else in middle or old age.

"The one thing a man cannot do," Chesterton tells us, "is exactly what all modern artists and free lovers are always trying to do. He cannot cut his life into separate sections." We cannot separate what we did yesterday from what we are doing right now or what we will do tomorrow. Our deeds have consequences in all the time in which we are. This is why we have memories. What is called "modern love," Chesterton tells us, makes the claim to do this, to separate what we do on Thursday or in April from what we do on Friday or in December. "You cannot have an idyll with Maria and an episode with Jane; there is no such thing as an episode." The reason for this blunt affirmation is that Maria talks to Jane. Life cannot be so compartmentalized as if we are living in totally air-tight worlds.

Thus, "it is idle to talk about abolishing the tragedy of marriage when you cannot abolish the tragedy of sex." All our real commitments are "irrevocable." To pretend otherwise is never to know what either marriage or sex are. We can, of course, go ahead and cut our lives up into sections, into "idylls" and "episodes," as Chesterton called them. But in so doing, we will soon discover that life does not allow us to forget the relation of one idyll to another episode. Thus, "the *basis of tragedy* is that man lives a coherent and continuous life." That is to say, his acts carry through to the end that they establish for themselves.

We are free to act or not to act, but not so free that our acts have no consequences. "Man… has always this characteristic of physical and psychological unity. His identity continues long enough to see the end of many of his own acts; he cannot be cut off from his past with a hatchet." We can never escape our past, though we can be forgiven our sins, provided we recognize that we committed them. We remain the ones who caused them and what flows from them in a complete life. Forgiven sins do not cease to be a part of our very selves and their consequences remain in the world.

Chesterton, in this essay, uses Macbeth as the example of what he means. Macbeth tried to act as if he could cut up his life in episodes. He could, he thought, commit one terrible act and live the rest of his life in peace and nobility. Macbeth seems legitimately destined for power. But suddenly he sees a shortcut to more power. Duncan is what prevents him from being elevated to the Crown of Scotland. Therefore, get rid of Duncan and he will be content. "If he does that one cruel thing he can be infinitely kind and happy." Such is the classic thesis of the disordered soul.

This principle, of course, is Machiavelli, the end justifying the means. Man can commit the one act, then forget it. He will live as if it never happened. He will not worry about it. The same thinking, I suspect, happens to many who obtain abortions thinking that the one "cruel act" will be the ticket to a contented life afterward. In fact, life becomes a remorseless memory of what "might have been," what should have been. It will not be simply "forgotten," no more than Macbeth could forget his dastardly deed.

Chesterton elucidates the principle as follows: "You cannot do a mad thing in order to reach sanity." This position is reminiscent of Socrates' "it is never right to do wrong." When Macbeth goes ahead with his terrible deed, his character remains. Indeed, "the crime does not get rid of the problem. Its effect is so bewildering that one may say that the crime does not get rid of the temptation." That is, the whole scene, the initial concoction and its being carried out, remains in our memories through all the stages of our subsequent lives, particularly so in the case of crimes that are not forgiven, especially in a world that rejects the very notion of forgiveness. Even forgiven ones remain, of course, but now as acknowledged for what they are. We do not pretend they are virtues, as happens in so much of modernity. We no longer hide ourselves from ourselves. "Do a lawless thing and you will only get into an atmosphere much more suffocating than that of law."

Chesterton's conclusion to this very brief but profound essay is nothing short of brilliant: "For us moderns, therefore, the first philosophical significance of the play (Macbeth) is this: that our life is one thing and that our lawless acts limit us; every time we break a law we make a limitation. In some strange way hidden in the deeps of human psychology, if we build our palace on some unknown wrong, it turns very slowly into our prison." Our lives are wholes, not separate episodes. We love to make them whole again, even with the episodes and idylls, if we be sane. We can do this, but not by ourselves. It is not by accident that our restored wholeness, if we achieve it, is via the Cross of someone else. "Every time we break a law, we make a limitation." This is why our freedom is not in breaking the law, but in keeping it.

Chapter 9

Truth as a Reality

On February 10, 2006, Benedict XVI received his old Congregation for the Doctrine of the Faith colleagues (*L'Osservatore Romano*, English, February 22). The Pope here broached the noblest issues of our kind. Many things were succinctly put together that are not often put together, succinctly or otherwise. Catholics, almost anywhere, can address the highest things concretely.

"Faith has a fundamental importance in the life of the Church, because the gift that God makes of himself in Revelation is fundamental and God's gift of himself is accepted through faith." Fully to know what we are, faith is needed. Faith comes through the Church, affirming that God has given Himself to us.

What happens when this "centrality of the Catholic faith" weakens? In 1968, Eric Voegelin wrote that the major cause of ideology was the weakening of faith in Christian men who, as a result, try to relocate transcendent ends of Christian life in movements in this world. The "last things" became "immanentized," a memorable but dense word.

Similarly, Benedict XVI observes: "Whenever the perception of this centrality weakens, the fabric of ecclesial life loses its original brightness…: it degenerates into static activism or is reduced to political expediency with a worldly fl vor." This "reduction" is what has happened. "Faith" becomes "justice." Justice becomes ideology. Ideology, exclusively with the human mind, explains the world solely from within the world.

But charity leads to and from faith. The Pope cites *Deus Caritas Est* (#1): "Being Christian is not the result of an ethical choice or a lofty idea, but the encounter with an event, a person, which gives life a new horizon and a decisive direction." Aristotle had affirmed that we cannot find truth if our moral life is disordered. What Christianity adds is that we will not have our moral life ordered without a gift from outside of ourselves, something that Plato himself intimated. The difference is that we, following Aquinas, can give a description of what this gift is like because it has been first given to us, not of our own making.

Truth is not an abstraction. "Jesus Christ is the Personified Truth who attracts the world to himself.... Every other truth is a fragment of the Truth that he is, and refers to him." We first encounter a person. We do not think up an idea. But from the Person encountered flow all the truths that we naturally and passionately seek more fully to know.

"*Truth (is) offered as a reality* that restores the human being and at the same time surpasses him and towers above him, as a Mystery that embraces and at the same time exceeds the impulse of his intelligence." What happens to philosophy and human knowledge here? Neither is denied or denigrated but accepted for what each is. We see an openness to a truth sought, not yet known. "Nothing succeeds as well as love for the truth in impelling the human mind towards unexplored horizons." Here are found the "restless hearts" of Augustine pounding in ears of today.

"Truth alone can take possession of the mind and make it rejoice to the full." *Joy is the possession of what we love.* "This joy... moves and attracts the human person to free adoration, not to servile prostration but to bow with heartfelt respect before the Truth he has encountered." Might this passage, one wonders, refer to what Cardinal Ratzinger once said about the Divine Liturgy in Santa Sophia during the time of the Kiev emissaries contrasted with the same place after the Fall of Byzantium?

Service follows as a grace from this love and adoration, not vice versa. And science? "The great progress of scientific knowledge that we saw during the last century has helped us to understand the mystery of Creation better and has profoundly marked the awareness of all peoples." Is "intrinsic design" thus not totally irrational? "Every study that aims to deepen the knowledge of the truths discovered by reason is vitally important, in the certainty that there is not 'competition of any kind between reason and faith.'" (*F/R*, #17). *Catholic talk is things-fit-together talk.*

Christ is the "center of the cosmos and history." The dialogue of faith and reason shows men of our time the "reasonableness of faith in God." It "demonstrates (that) the definitive fulfillment of every authentic human aspiration rests in Jesus Christ." Faith is not "against" reason; therefore we can talk of such "demonstration."

"The desire for the truth is part of human nature itself. The whole of creation is an immense invitation to seek those responses that open human reason to the great response that it has always sought and awaited." As I say, when he welcomes his old friends, the Pope talks of the highest things.

Chapter 10

Always a Gift

The day after Easter, I was rereading Benedict XVI's new and brilliant encyclical, *Spe Salvi*. I have three different copies of this remarkable document, one printed from the Vatican on-line system, one from *L'Osservatore Romano*, in English, and a bound version published by Pauline Books. I was reading this latter publication when, as often happens, I ran across a sentence that did not strike me the earlier times I had read this encyclical.

This is the sentence: *"Heaven is always more than we could merit, just as being loved is never something 'merited,' but always a gift"* (#35).

What struck me here was the analogy between heaven-merit and love-merit. Behind this issue stands the whole controversy in the Reformation about whether we could by ourselves "merit" salvation by our "works." The orthodox doctrine, of course, is that we cannot "merit" salvation as such. If we could, we would already be gods in no need of it.

But if heaven is "more" than we could merit, it still may be offered to us but nogt initially as a result of merit. This is the ultimate surprise of what it is to be a human being, that both heaven and love are offered to us as a gift, probably because they are the same thing. Nor does it mean that we cannot "merit" anything as a result of our own deeds. It is just that first we must be graced before we even think of doing something that may be meritorious of our final end. Indeed, such a gift incites us to do what is meritorious to others. With it, we can and will do things that we would not otherwise either think of or carry out.

The other side of the analogy has to do with love, which is the basis of redemption as we know it in the first place. We must be careful to catch the nuances here. If we are "loved," – not love, but *are loved* – it is always a "gift," not just in heaven. Being loved is not a response to our good looks, such as they be, to our brains, brawn, income, clout or virtues. These may be the occasions for our being noticed by someone.

Such qualities are not what it is ultimately that is loved. That is to say, if someone really loves us, it is not principally because of something we do to make us worthy, even if we should strive to be worthy. Love essentially makes us worthy by first penetrating to the core of what we are.

It is said that if we are not first loved, something we have first received, we will never be able to love someone else. The familial and personal status of every human being is bound up with this principle. That is, if we think that the object of love is our worthiness caused by something we do, we will never really be loved for what we are. This is why both heaven and love have to be free, and for the same reason. They are both first gifts.

The concept of a "gift" is one of the most profound ideas of our existence. It goes against practically everything in our culture that constructs the world on the basis of "rights," on what is first "due" to us from someone else. If we spend our lives defining and demanding our "rights," chances are we will never be much loved, even though there may still be those who love us none the less. We will think that we can demand love. We can accuse those of fault who do not choose to love us. I cannot think of a sadder assumption than this.

A gift is not essentially the "what is given," the flowers, the box of candy. First, it is rather a human effort to concretize, make incarnate, something that is spiritual and invisible, yet real and bodily. If we like our gifts because they are expensive, we probably do not know what the love of the giver is, nor what heaven is for that matter.

This view, however, does not mean that expensive gifts are essentially alienations. Quite the contrary, gifts also have that quality of being sacrificial. The sentimental stories of the little boy who works all summer to give his mother a twenty dollar gift, instead of buying something for himself, also are symbolic of the nature of a real gift. There is no reason that a very wealthy man may not give expensive gifts because he in fact loves someone. But everyone who loves can and indeed should at times give gifts. This is itself a sign that, among us, love is already incarnate, already has taken flesh.

"Heaven is always more than we could merit, just as being loved is never something 'merited,' but always a gift."

The foundations of the world are not based in justice. There is something more than justice, without denying that justice has its place. There can be, and usually are, those who love us in spite of the fact that we do our best to be un-lovable. But once we know that we are loved, it is a virtue to do all we can for those we ourselves love. The first-being-loved is itself a powerful force for knowledge and action.

Love is always a "gift," and as such it is unmerited. The whole of the physical and human cosmos is based on this truth. We ourselves exist first as gifts. The first metaphysical question that we need to ask ourselves is whether we are the sole origin of what is gift-worthy in us. If we think we are, we will never understand the universe *that is*.

Chapter 11

Schall at Eighty

Schall was born on January 20, 1928, on a farm in Pocahontas County, Iowa. You cannot get more "American" than that. My mother was Bohemian and my father German/Irish. To my Jesuit colleagues at breakfast on my birthday I hint that this memorable event happened in "a log cabin." Most doubt this as too picturesque, while others are sure Schall confuses himself with Abraham Lincoln.

Previously, I did columns on "Schall at Seventy" and "Schall at Seventy-Five." So the fates decree "Schall at Eighty." A wonderful old Jesuit died here this year at one hundred-and-five. You need not anticipate.

Of late, whenever I come across Psalm 90 in the Office, I do my calculations: "The years of our life are threescore and ten (70), or even by reason of strength fourscore (80)." Not bad but the next line reads: "Yet their span is but toil and trouble; they are soon gone, and we fly away." The "soon gone" is the very condition of human life. The Psalm is on target. "Toil and trouble" are known.

In some educational journal, I saw an essay entitled, "The Aging Professorate." We are the only country in the world that by law allows people my age to continue to teach, provided we do not babble or otherwise show signs of dementia.

The ancients associated wisdom and age, as the name "Senate," a body of old, that is, wise, men implies. Are all the elderly, including Schall, therefore wise? Hardly.

Old age was the topic that began the conversation of Plato's *Republic*.

> "Indeed, Cephalus," Socrates says, "I enjoy talking with the very old, for we should ask them, as we might ask those who have traveled a road that we too will probably have to follow, what kind of road it is, whether rough and difficult or smooth and easy. And I'd gladly find out from you what you think about this, as you have

reached the point in life the poets call 'the threshold of old age' (Odyssey, xvi, 218). Is it a difficult time? What is your report about it?" (328d–e).

Yes, what does Schall "report" about it?

The Greeks thought that only the gods were wise. The philosopher sought wisdom but he would never be a god. "To know that he did not know" was the mark of the wise man. That is not a bad criterion, provided it is not a formula for skepticism.

The human mind is made to know, to know *what is*. One looks back with a certain amusement about what he knew at twenty or so, the same age as Schall's present students. I have of late been haunted by the following passage from book seven of the *Republic*.

"At present, those who study philosophy do so as young men who have just left childhood behind and have yet to take up household management and money-making," Socrates says.

> But just when these reach the hardest part – I mean the part that has to do with giving a rational account – they abandon it and are regarded as fully trained in philosophy. In later life, they think they're doing well if they are willing to be in an invited audience when others are doing philosophy, for they think they should do this only as a sideline. And, with few exceptions, by the time they reach old age, their eagerness for philosophy is quenched... (498a–b).

To study philosophy too soon is a dangerous occupation.

The most difficult part, as Socrates says, is "giving a rational account." I am struck by this phrase. It intimates that very few are philosophers. Recently, I have published a book entitled *The Regensburg Lecture*, concerning Benedict's reminder that the Christian faith is directed to *logos*, to reason which it needs and respects. Indeed, Christians from Chesterton to John Paul II maintain that the common man can know some philosophy. Often he is closer to the truth than the academic philosopher.

Yet, Plato is right. "The eagerness for philosophy" can be "quenched" or redirected away from *what is*. Of late, these things have interested me, the "rational account," that it is revelation that "cures" or completes reason. The work of reason is more often considered in the Church than in politics, more carefully considered too.

The year 2008 is the one-hundredth anniversary of Chesterton's

Orthodoxy, a book I dearly love. The book was twenty years old when I was born in a log cabin in Iowa. Chesterton too spoke of *what is*, proably the only thing worth talking about. It would be unnatural of Schall not to conclude with *Orthodoxy*.

"People have fallen into a foolish habit of speaking of orthodoxy as some thing heavy, humdrum, and safe. There never was anything so perilous or so exciting as orthodoxy. It was sanity: and to be sane is more dramatic than to be mad" (100). This is what Schall has to report at eighty. Both the peril and the excitement are there, for we are free. We are "sane," not "mad." We know the difference. For this, we give a "rational account," even at eighty.

Chapter 12

Three Books and Three Essays

Thomas Aquinas is known for being, at the same time, very terse and very diffusive. He can state the basic principles of *all that is* in a few brief, riveting Latin words. At the same time, he has no difficulty, in a short life, in writing volumes and volumes of fundamental principles on all phases of reality.

Those who know me are used to the fact that I am capable, at the drop of a hat, of recommending to them this book or that. I do so with great enthusiasm – "Read this!" A good book is a treasure. It is not an uncommon experience, when we read something that strikes us as particularly true or well-said or funny, to rush off looking for someone to whom to read it, almost as if what is ours is not ours until we give it to someone else.

It is my particular calling, I sometimes think, to be concerned with what I call "the life of the mind." I am aware that the disorders in the world stem mainly from the will, not the mind, even though a mind component is found in any disorder or sin. Often in my thoughts I mull over what I would recommend to someone who really wants to know the truth of things. What would I tell him? Where would I tell him to go? Whom should he consult? I have multi-lists of ten books, twenty books, twenty-five books. "Acquire these," I tell anyone who will listen.

I know about Scripture, Aquinas, Plato, Aristotle, Augustine, and the rest. I have long given out lists of what I call "minor" classics, books that no one tells us about in the university or in the culture, but books that nevertheless explain the essence and right order of things. At the top if this list is probably, for me, Chesterton. Nothing is quite like him. He makes truth so delightfully clear that we deliberately have to close our souls to keep it out as we read him. Chesterton is not someone to dally with if we want to hide our inner selves from truth.

What I have in mind here, however, is the following project. Let us suppose that someone wanted to read, say, but three books that would explain in clear, profound, and incisive terms the whole structure of human life, its destiny, how it stands before God and the world. What books would I recommend? Or if some parent asked me what three books should he give his son or daughter on the way to college, something that, if read and pondered, would keep *what is* clearly before his eyes, in all its philosophic and revelational dimensions, what books would these be? If some unsuspecting student inquires, what should I read this summer, what three books would I suggest?

Or if a young man or woman, out of college for several years, has suddenly become aware of how shallow his education had been, what would I recommend? Or suppose someone fifty or sixty, who has lived a practical and not always edifying life, was now prepared to look again at the truth square in the eyes, what would I recommend? Imagine some cleric or religious has finally realized the contemporary shallowness of his theological or philosophical background and wanted something at the same time profound and eminently clear and direct, what would I recommend?

For these purposes, which are after all the same, I would recommend three books, two of which are just on the market, one has been out since 1989, at least in English. Its German original, once given to me by a German student, was published in 1981.

Read carefully and leisurely together, these books give a better and more coherent overall picture of the unity of intellectual things, the relation of reason and revelation, the order of knowledge, the meaning of modern thought, of virtue and vice, than anything else that one could read, except perhaps Chesterton.

These three books are the following: 1) *Josef Pieper – an Anthology*. This is the German book. 2) Peter Kreeft, *The Philosophy of Tolkien*, and 3) Ralph McInerny, *The Very Rich Hours of Jacques Maritain: A Spiritual Life*. None of these books is very long. Each is relatively easy to read. All three are as profound as any book ever written. They all deal with *what is*.

These books cover every issue of any importance about how to live and what is true. Each of the authors knows classic and modern thought. None of these books intends to be apologetic; yet, taken together, they constitute the finest apologetic imaginable. They are all lyrical. They deal with evil. They take us to the order of things in a way that nothing else will in quite the same way. "Read them!"

Though this could go on forever, after I finished the essay on the three books, I wondered if there were not three essays that I could add that would re-enforce the three books. I would suggest these three: 1) Benedict XVI, "The Regensburg Lecture," 2) Robert Sokolowski's heavy-sounding but penetrating "Phenomenology and the Eucharist," in his *Christian Faith & Human Understanding*, and 3) Hans Urs von Balthasar's "Resume of My Thought," in *Communio* (March 1988). I do not know a faster or more penetrating way to acquire a knowledge of the whole than through reading these three books and these three essays.

Chapter 13

The Enormity of the Universe

Should the vast size of the universe concern us? Could indeed we fail to notice it? We have researchers trying to give us some estimate of its distance in terms of light years and billions of years in the making. Pascal, in a famous passage, said that the infinite spaces of the heavens frightened him. Why did they not exhilarate him? Space is not so overwhelming if we have reasons to think that it had a creator.

Yet, one of the reasons why people do not want the universe to be created, even if it is created, is because of what it implies. It suggests that a reason can be given for its existence, size and all. Further, this reason may just have something to do with ourselves. That is, we may not be just an afterthought in the whole system, as if we were utterly insignificant. A quick way out of the implications of personal responsibility, then, is simply to deny any meaning at all either to the universe or to ourselves within it.

That leaves us supposedly "free" but, at the same time, meaningless, except for any possible meaning we might give ourselves, a meaning that is not particularly consoling. Actually, this denial of an intelligent origin of things usually does not leave us free either. Rather it leaves us stuck in a determined universe that is doing what it must do. We are as a result anything but free.

I often find philosophic principles in unexpected places. Linus and Charlie Brown are standing on a knoll; the darkest of nights surrounds them. While gazing into the mysterious night sky, Charlie says to Linus, "Have you ever considered *the enormity of the universe*, Linus?" The question is definitely a new one for Linus, who clearly has not thought of it.

In the next scene, with his arms wide as if taking it all in, Charlie continues, "Nobody knows what lies out there beyond the stars." This very observation suggests that we do wonder about what is "beyond the stars." The third scene has no words. In awe, both Charlie and Linus continue to stand and stare at the dark night. Finally, Linus, obviously reflecting on the enormity question, says to Charlie, "I don't even know what's in the next block."

Both the enormity of the universe and what is going on in the next block can be, perhaps ought to be, of concern to us. Our minds, Aristotle said, are capable of knowing all things. We just do not have time in this life to get around to them all, but we would like to if we could. That very curious fact may be one of the reasons why we wonder about the given insufficiency of this life to cover *all that is*. Why do we have such a power to know, which evidently comes first to be fully aware of itself in our early twenties? It is a power that requires more for its flourishing than we can possibly have time for in one lifetime. It seems like a natural invitation to frustration. There are not a few who take it as such.

I have often asked the question of myself, "Why is it all right to be a human being?" You may wonder what Schall is mumbling about when you see him walking across campus! But a turtle does not ask himself, "Why is it all right to be a turtle?" – or at least I have never met one that did. But a human being who does not ask himself such a question of himself, by implication, is failing to be a human being. We are peculiar kinds of beings. We not only are, but want to know what we are, why we are. For us, it is not enough just to exist.

Yves Simon makes a very insightful remark in this regard. The only way that we can be the kind of being we are, the one that does not even know what is going on in the next block, is for us not to be anything else but ourselves, but what we are. This means, logically, that I want what is not myself to be precisely "not myself." The *enormity of the universe* is not, somehow, opposed to the obvious particularity in the universe. Indeed, the power of intellect seems to suggest that, in the end, I am really not deprived of what is not myself. If I set myself to it, I can know what is not myself. Indeed, this endeavor to know what is not myself seems to be what I am supposed to do.

Well, this is heavy stuff. But in the *enormity of the universe* I do not want anyone to forget Linus's earnest realization, that he didn't even know what is going on in the next block. It is amazing what we do not know about what is going on next door. We do not in fact want anyone to know everything about ourselves or we them unless we love them.

What is the conclusion to all this reflection on everything and every thing? In his *Lost in the Cosmos*, a title not wholly related to the *enormity of the universe*, Walker Percy asked the following pertinent ques- tion: "Why is it possible to learn more in ten minutes about the Crab Nebula in Taurus, which is 6,000 light-years away, than you presently know about yourself, even though you've been living with yourself all your life?" As I say, the universe is enormous and we are in it. Both the enormity of the universe and what is going on in the next block can be, perhaps ought to be, of interest to us. It may of course be mere babbling to think of these things, or it may finally be a sign that you have begun to wonder about *what is*, including about yourself and what goes on in the next block.

Chapter 14

The One Good Thing to Do with Money

Collections of letters can be charming. One of the things I like best about them, and I like this about journals and essay collections also, is that they can be so random. One's day is not usually an organized treatise in which one thing flows directly from another in some logical patter. I have nothing against logic or organization, but I rather like to live in a world in which I am not quite sure what will happen next. I like it when folks can just "drop by." The end of my world will come when weather forecasting becomes an exact science.

Such thoughts occurred to me in reading *The Correspondence of Shelby Foote and Walker Percy*, which I believe Scott Walter gave to me several years ago.[1] In a letter to Percy, dated April 5, 1975, from Memphis, Foote explains that he had just returned from New York City. On return, he finds on his desk *The Mississippi Quarterly* with reviews of books by both himself and Percy. But he is anxious to tell Percy what he did in the Big City. "We did as I said we would in NY," he explains, "ate our heads off – Lutece, La Fayette, San Marco, Caravelle, we did them all in style and at incredible expense without regret. Finally found one good thing to do with money: eat it, preferably with sauce Bercy and heavy drafts of Chateau Palmer or Gevrey-Chambertin. You only go round once, they say, but we went round several times in just four days" (203). *The one good thing to do with money – eat it!* Obviously, Foote knew what to eat, however "incredibly expensive." But if one is going to splurge this way in style, there can be "no regrets." Foote is right. It is not quite true that we go round only once – several times in four days. With the names of classy restaurants in New York and fine French wines given for our edification, we cannot but be amused by such delight with life itself. This lightsomeness is the way of friends with one another.

---

1 *The Correspondence of Shelby Foote and Walker Percy*, edited by Jay Tolson (New York: Norton, 1997).

Several days later, April 8, Percy replies. He expects Foote to receive the Pulitzer Prize, but he never heard of *The Mississippi Review*. He tells Foote that he does not mind criticism, which Foote had noted in *The Mississippi Review*. "Praise always makes me feel vaguely guilty, as well as bored." Percy had been teaching courses in college. In a year he would be sixty and Foote would be sixty-one. This fact precipitated reflection on retirement, on ultimate things. "So what now? It is a question of desire, what one wants to do – write something better or run off with two girls to the islands. Having delivered the last word on the nature of man, I am in a quandary." How amusing is this passage from the author of *Lost in the Cosmos*. The irony of reaching retirement is to wonder what to do next, as if there were a "next." How could one who has "delivered the last word on the nature of man" still be in a "quandary?" What if the last word is that there is no last word – what then? Write some more? Run off to the islands? Do these alternatives solve the "quandary" about the "nature of man?" They never did before. Percy laughs at his own irony.

On May 5, Foote writes back to Percy. He talks about his reading of Dante. "What amazed me was my reaction once I put the Inferno behind me. I had thought that once he got out of hell the story would sag into banality. I couldnt (sic) have been wronger (sic). The Purgatory was exciting beyond belief – and, though I couldnt really compass it without the theological background, I could see that the Paradise would be the best of all for someone prepared to appreciate it" (209). Foote and Percy at times "spell" somewhat Southern to each other, of course – "couldnt," "wronger." This passage again tells of the surprise that joy is more riveting than gore and horror. He tells Percy that he can find the book and commentaries in the LSU Library. "All Dante ever wrote about was Love, and once you understand that, you will read him with an immediacy that outdoes Faulkner or Hopkins or anyone else on the list…" (210). This is right, I think, the excitement of the good far surpasses the attraction of evil.

Evidently, in a previous letter, Percy has cryptically said something to Foote about the ultimate consequences of his not being a Catholic. Foote's response is most witty. "I'm sorry to learn from your letter that you and F. (Flannery) O'Connor wont be joining me in heaven – I presume that's what you meant when you said that two of us three wouldnt be making it" (211). In these celestial calculations, a barb can cut both ways. Foote implies that, not Flannery or Percy, but he himself will miss them both when he is in this happy place that Dante describes so well.

Foote keeps returning to Dante. He compares him to James Joyce in a curious manner. He does not think Joyce up to the level of Dante, though "he's (Joyce) just the best we've got" – presumably in English. However, both Joyce and Dante have something in common. "Fierce haters, both, great payers-off of scores and both with ice water in their veins when they wanted to score the wicked who had crossed them." The Inferno is liberally populated with the powerful of church and world. The ice water is needed, as retaliation can be expected to be swift.

In a letter of June 30, Foote is still thinking of Dante. He has Percy now also reading Dante. Foote found bits of the Inferno and Purgatorio in Faulkner and Celine. He understood those lower scenes quite well – "the meaning of life amidst the squalor" (214). It was the Comedy itself that was the new form of literature. This is not what he was prepared for. "Only in the Paradise did I get a feeling of being out of my depth, and even there I had an overwhelming feeling of being involved in the very greatest conception of them all; the windup mystical rose, the love that moves the stars, all that." It is not stars that move stars, nor is it ultimately only the forces of nature that move us. At the roots of all motion lies a reality that moves by loving, that moves by being loved.

Finally, on July 26, Foote figures that Percy is about half-way through his reading of the Inferno. He warns him not to stop in the fourth terrace of Hell wherein the sin of sloth is punished. Then Foote adds, surprisingly, a comment from Thomas Aquinas – "Aquinas identifies sloth as a form of *sadness*" (215). The word sadness is in italics, to emphasize its importance.

Josef Pieper has also made much of this word *acedia*, sloth. It does not mean, as we might expect, laziness. Rather it means that we refuse seriously to examine what we are, what kind of being we are, because we do not want to know, lest we have to face the conduct of our lives in terms of *what is*, and not just what we would like. Perhaps, Foote is humorously telling Percy and F. O'Connor that if they want to join him in heaven, they best be moving through to the Comedy that is Divine.

This exhortation on love in Dante does not deny that the best thing we can do with money is, as Foote says, to "eat it," especially in style at "incredibly expensive" restaurants in New York, with exceptional French wine, but emphatically "no regrets." We are to enjoy what exists to be enjoyed. Still, it does remind us, in the course of ordinary letter writing, that we can come across astonishing things there, that paradise is much more astonishing than hell or purgatory ever thought to be. Having "delivered the last word on the nature of man" and not taken off to the islands, perhaps we need not be in so much of a "quandary," when we realize, as Dante tells us, that "it is love that moves the stars, all that." Of such things, we come across in books of letters.

Chapter 15

The Power of Great Minds

What is peculiar to Catholicism is that, while it is a religion of intellect, it is also concerned with the salvation of lesser luminaries, of ordinary folks, even of those with no functioning intelligence. The aborted fetus, who is given no chance, has the same transcendent destiny as the greatest philosopher, or the greatest sinner. Indeed, the greatest philosopher and the greatest sinner may be, to recall Lucifer, the same person. The distinction between the intelligent and the normal is worthy and not to be disdained, but it is not a distinction of kind. As both the rich and the poor can save their souls or lose them, so the brainy and the slow. We are not Gnostics claiming that our destiny depends on a secret doctrine closed to all but the wise.

Such thoughts are occasioned by a sermon (#2 on the Ascension) of St. Leo the Great. "For such is *the power of great minds*," Leo wrote, "such the light of truly believing souls, that they put unhesitating faith in what is not seen with the bodily eye; they fix their desires on what is beyond sight. Such fidelity could never be born in our hearts, nor could anyone be justified by faith, if our salvation lay only in what was visible." The distinction between what is visible and what is invisible is not a distinction between what is real and what is not real.

Many invisible things are real. E. F. Schumacher gives as an example the inner life of another person. What I see when I see others is their exterior, but I realize that, in knowing this exterior, I know little about that person. To know someone else, I not only have to know myself, but freely to be given access to another's soul. That opening does not depend on me. This access is what freedom, love, and friendship are about.

Josef Cardinal Ratzinger, in his essay, "Faith and Theology," put it well: "If the form of verification of modern natural science were the only way in which man could arrive at any certainty, then faith would indeed have to be classified in the realm of mere 'perhaps….' But just as a person becomes certain of another's love without being able to subject it to the methods of scientific experiment, so with the contact between God and man...." A scientific method measures only what it is designed to measure. What it does not measure still exists.

In *Gravity and Grace*, Simon Weil remarked that "we know by means of our intelligence that what the intelligence does not comprehend is more real than what it does."

This comment indicates, as St. Leo said, "the power of a great mind." The point of this passage, however, depends on the fact that the mind, the intelligence, does comprehend something. It does not begin in nothingness, but with itself and with *what is*.

We could not be "justified by faith" if everything we needed to know were to be seen by our "bodily eyes." When we read such a comment, in thinking about the intellect in general, we are tempted to imagine that the real "me" is essentially an abstract mind. Spiritual beings do exist. We are not one of these types of being. The doctrine of the resurrection of the body itself forever banishes such positions from our minds. Still, we have minds and we are expected to use them. The mind is a power of our soul. In itself, it is indeed "immortal," but this bodiless condition is neither its natural nor final condition.

In his *Lost Lectures*, Maurice Baring wrote an essay on "The Nineties" – meaning the 1890's, the famous "Gay Nineties." "If you had told people then (1890's)," Baring wrote, "that in 1931 Verdi would be more popular than Wagner among the young... they would not have believed you: 'believed' is a mild word; they would have thought you stark staring mad."

These words "belief," "intelligence," and "madness" are related. Pope Leo had no difficulty in relating belief, not to lack of intelligence, but precisely to its presence. Simone Weil, closer to our time, reaffirmed the same. Baring was aware that even unanticipated changes of taste could be called "mad." Faith too is often called "mad" to obscure its real relation to "the power of great minds."

Chapter 16

On What Not to Forget

Fifty years hence, if you are still in this world, you will recall your first confused week here at Georgetown University. The campus's most striking physical aspect, I think, is not its size. Nor is it its federal location above the Potomac. What is most striking clearly is the dark-stoned Healy Building with its slender towers. Without this building, Georgetown, as we know it, would not be Georgetown even though Georgetown was here before this building by almost a hundred years.

The older and newer brick buildings out-number the stone constructions of Copley, White-Gravenor, and Healy. The red hues of campus brick are often splendid against the green and the spring cherry blossoms. But the Healy Building and its main tower serve to rivet the place in our vision and eventually in our memories.

My purpose here is not a history of this lofty building, its so-called "Flemish Gothic." Anyone whose soul is not moved by it, in my view, has no soul. When and from where the vision of Healy is best viewed can be debated. I have seen it in the winter looking up "O" Street between leafless branches. Nothing is more beautiful than the Healy Building during a misty January falling snow. But when the trees in its front – they might be crab-apple – bloom deep reddish purple blossoms, it is simply lovely in the early spring sun.

Often I see the Healy Building while walking in the morning when the sun rises low in the brightening sky from Georgetown. The front of the building basks in the radiant light. The evening sun from the Chapel Quadrangle gives yet another memorable vista. From the Jesuit building on the lower campus, I cannot normally see the main tower. But the slimmer tower on the Lauinger Library side makes our walk simply elegant.

Strolling back to campus on "N" Street, I often watch the Clock Tower. The seasons give the building different moods. I have also come onto the campus late at night, especially when we Jesuits lived in the old buildings across from Dahlgren Chapel. Sometimes, on the way in, you could catch the full moon just above the Tower. We would enter our residence from the door under the main tower, so you could look straight up at it from below, with the soft lights of the Clock. I have even seen the Clock minus its hands. Some daring, mountain-climbing student managed to detach them – a practice not to be recommended, though I cannot help but admire anyone with skill and guts enough to accomplish such a feat.

I have not had a class in the Healy Building in recent years. I do not, in fact, like those bank-type classrooms that remain on the first floor. They are not conducive to my style of teaching. In its upper floors, students used to reside, but now are found mainly office-space for university bureaucracy, no small operation, to be sure.

Whether a more beautiful academic salon can be found in Washington than Gaston Hall, I doubt. Foreign potentates and U.S. politicians like to speak here as this Hall is a classic of its type: right size, right ambience, looks great on TV. The Philodemic Room, next to the President's Office, is also quite charming, as is the President's Office itself and the Hall of Jesuit Cardinals. Sooner or later, you should manage a peek in these rooms. The staff is usually very accommodating, especially if your parents are visiting from Peoria.

In local art galleries, you will often see paintings of the view downriver from Key Bridge looking back at the Healy Building, usually with stalwart youth rowing. The walk back from Rosslyn on Key Bridge always is breath-taking not only of the vistas, up and down river, but also of the Healy Building itself. Actually the Library Tower, evidently designed to imitate the Healy Towers, though itself no Healy Tower, does not look at all bad from the river over against the Healy Spires.

What am I saying here? That place is a real category of being, as Aristotle said. It is quite possible to live in a beautiful place but never notice, just as it is possible to be taught or read something true, but no impression is left on our soul. Still, a beautiful place, like a beautiful person, cannot stand a lot of explanation.

Aquinas said that the definition of beauty is simply "*quod visum, placet.*" A university can only do so much for you. Some things must simply be experienced, usually the noblest and most profound things. "The best things in life are free," as they say. So are the most beautiful ones, if we just notice them, there on the horizon above Potomack's Waters.

Chapter 17

Unlike the Spider in the Window:
"To Chuse, Is to Do"

Composed between 1604 and 1608, we have four letters, seven text-pages total, that John Donne, the English poet and divine, wrote to his friend, Sir Henry Goodyer. The edition I have (Modern Library, 1952) retains the earlier spellings. In the first letter (52 lines). Donne mentions Pliny, St. Paul, Seneca, "the Jesuites," the "Evangiles and Acts," a supposed letter from Christ ("our B. Saviour") to King Agabarus, Michael Montaigne, and the Roman poet, "Martiall." Donne concludes with a delightful discussion of Roman matrons.

The letter begins, however, with a remarkable passage explaining what letters are about in the first place. Evidently, Donne is a frequent correspondent, so much so that he has to explain to Sir Henry why he writes so often. "If you were here," he tells him, "you would not think me importune, if I bid you a good morning every day." If Sir Henry understands this analogy between daily politeness and frequent letters, Sir Henry's "patience" will excuse "my often Letters."

But since this very series is designed to keep our attention focused on the importance and charm of letters and essays in our literature, I was more than delighted by Donne's next sentence: "No other kind of conveyance is better for knowledge, or love." The frequent letter conveys better than anything else both knowledge and love – what greater encomium could we have of letters!

To prove his point, Donne recalls Seneca's letters – the one to *Lucilius* alone proves his point, he thinks. Pliny's letters tell of natural knowledge. Cicero's letters told a great deal of "the storie of the time." Presumably referring to the famous "Relations," that is, accounts of Jesuits in missions in the orient and the New World, he finds in them much of "all these times." Donne mentions the notorious character of Phalaris, by all accounts the worst of ancient tyrants whose own letters "are about so many writs of Execution."

Considering them also to be mainly letters, Donne tells us that "the Evangiles and Acts, teach us what to believe, but the Epistles of the Apostles what to do." No small helps, these. Donne thought that Seneca was over-rated so someone dreamed up a fake correspondence between Seneca, the Stoic philosopher, and St. Paul, who does know of the Stoics. This correspondence, presumably, would enhance Seneca's stature.

The fact is, however, the prize for letter-writing goes, perhaps with some irony, to the Italians. The Italians "think the world owes them all wisdom." He recalls that Montaigne "saies that he hath seen, (as I remember) 400 volumes of Italian Letters." But Donne thinks that letters are in fact "the best conveyers of love." Yet, even if there is this wisdom in letters, it means nothing unless it is read and pondered. "Much of the knowledge buried in Books perished, and became ineffectual, if it be not applied, and refreshed by a companion, or friend." Our wisdom is not alive if we have no one with whom to communicate it.

Donne compares our interest in letters to the bite of the "Tarentola" which seems to bother us only for a moment, according to "physicians of Italy." We correspond with live authors, but if they are dead, even if we have "a boxe" of such letters in our Library, we won't read them. (Such are not the words of an archivist!) We can discuss with a living writer what he means in his letters, but when dead we can only "beleeve, or discredit." Something is irretrievably lost in death, no doubt, even in letters of the dead.

Donne reflects that now that he is writing to Sir Henry and is now "upon the stage," he finds that he has nothing profound to say. Which is just as well, as the letter is already "too long" – it is about a page.

Donne worries about "the probleme supply" of words if a letter is too long. It seems that Sir Henry had worried about ladies not reading works that lacked "cleanlinesse." Donne turns the issue around by recalling the Roman epigramist Martial, who apparently used the following psychology to get Roman Matrons to read "Books which he thinks most morall and cleanly." The way to do this trick, Martial thought, was to put in the first epigram a notice to the potential reader to "skip the Book, because it was obscene." This sage system, evidently, guarantees a wide readership. Donne's advice is "either you write not at all for women, or for those of sincere palates."

Evidently, what worried Donne was that Sir Henry understand that he is not to give out Donne's privately printed *Problems* until he

(Donne) had a chance to review them or at least to know to whom they were sent. And this very prohibition, it seems, might have been, like the epigram for the Roman Matrons, a device to be sure everyone would read them.

In his letter to Sir Henry in September 1608, from his home in Mitchum, Donne, in a more sober mood, told him that every Thursday he turns a great hourglass that evidently measured exactly one week of time. This weekly turning gave Donne occasion to reflect on the passingness of things, of what he did last week and would do the next. Yet, we must do something. "But if I ask myself what I have done in the last watch, or would do in the next, I can say nothing; if I say that I have passed it without hurting any (one), so may the Spider in my window." That is, we are not here to do nothing. It is not a compliment to say of someone, week after week, that "he did nothing."

And this, finally, is the sentence that makes these short letters to Sir Henry worth detailed study: "For to chuse, is to do: but to be no part of any body, is to be nothing." These are Donne's powerful words about action. We are not made to be "nothing," but to "chuse," to "act." The spider in the window passed the week without hurting anyone. This is not the Hippocratic oath, "do no harm," but a statement of inertness, of being affected by nothing. We are made to choose. If we are really part of nothing, we are nothing. I found all of this in a letter of John Donne to Sir Henry Goodyer. "No other kind of conveyance is better for knowledge, or love." *To choose is to do.*

Chapter 18

Baring's Eton

Years ago, I remember reading Maurice Baring's (1874–1945) book *Lost Lectures*. I remember being highly amused by it, but I could not really recall anything in it. I always thought it would be nice to reread this book, but I never actually got around to it. However, a friend of mine, Jim Campbell, was somehow in London. I must have said something to him about Baring, because recently he sent me a copy of *Lost Lectures*, from 1932, which he had found in some used book store.

The book is marvelously amusing. Baring came from a famous English banking family. He never married. He became a Catholic in 1909. He was a British diplomat with much experience in Russia, reported the Russo-Japanese War, and was with the British Air Corps in World War I. He wrote of Russian novelists, also several novels of his own, and his autobiography. He was said by all who knew him to have been a very nice man. Joseph Epstein, making the same point, wrote a very good essay in the *New Criterion* (October, 1992) entitled, "Maurice Baring & the Good High-Brow." Lady Lovat, Paul Horgan, Joseph Pearce, among others, have written of this man of letters, a man whom even Marshal Foch, the famous French military leader, praised.

What interests me here, however, are Baring's recollections of his high school years at Eton, the famous English prep school in Windsor, whose list of graduates is itself a lesson in British history. Baring seems to have remembered every one of his six years there, plus all the teachers, the headmaster, the games, the classes, the ambience. Baring, who was there from his 13th to his 18th year, after which he went to Cambridge, was unabashedly happy at Eton. He has nothing but good to say about it. This is the value of his chapter on Eton in his *Lost Lectures*. "About my own experiences and my own feelings with regard to Eton I have no doubt whatsoever I enjoyed Eton whole-heartedly and unreservedly: I enjoyed it all from the first to the last moment."[1]   One can envy a man who can honestly write such lines. Baring was a delighted fan of Eton sporting crews and games. He never wanted Rugby, Winchester, or Harrow to win. "I believe that Eton has been and always will be the best school, and that there is none like her, none" (20).

One might wonder whether Baring as a boy had any critical sense at all. He tells us, however, that "it was the faults (of Eton) I liked best" (19). Of course, by including this chapter on Eton in *Lost Lectures*, while at the same time revealing so many foibles of the place, he sees even its sins as part of its charm. Indeed in seeing them, he includes, with all its humor, the human condition itself, about which we must learn or nothing else will be important.

"It is true," Baring writes. "It is true. Quite true. Games at Eton are all important." These games are played on the famous fields to which one of its graduates, the Duke of Wellington, is supposed to have attributed the victory over Napoleon. "The Battle of Waterloo was won on the playing fields of Eton." Baring often returns, ironically, to this theme. The chapel of the school, whose foundations go back to the Lancastrian dynasty, did not overshadow these fields. "Moralists have pointed out," he writes, "the sad fact that on Sundays in chapel the boys are taught to turn the other cheek, not to compete, to like the lowest place best. On Monday morning until Saturday evening they are told to strain every nerve to take the highest place, to compete with every nerve in their bodies, to aim at the highest place for the House, for the school, and for themselves, in every direction and in every respect, all day and in every way" (22).

Nietzsche, about this same time in Switzerland, writing of the dire effect of Christianity on his "superman," would have been confused by such lines. "They are no philosophical race – these English.... It is characteristic of such an un-philosophic race that they should cling firmly to Christianity – they need its discipline, if they are to become 'moral' and 'humane'" (*Beyond Good and Evil*, #252). Obviously, poor Nietzsche, as he penned these witty lines, did not know what was going on in either chapel or playing fields at Eton!

But not only did Christian values take a second place to sports, so too did academic honors. The winner of the "Hervey prize for English

---

1   Maurice Baring, *Lost Lectures or The Fruits of Experience* (London: Peter Davies, 1932).

verse" or the "Jelf prize for Latin verse" was no match in schoolboy honors to the "Captain of the Eleven" or the white flannels of the "Captain of the Boat." But Baring makes a very unexpected conclusion from these reflections on gamesmanship at Eton. "The beauty of the existing system is that the worship and importance of games gives those who did not excel in games, or who are fond, if not of study, of books, the leisure and the opportunity to cultivate their own tastes" (23). Baring included himself in this latter happy group. I particularly like that distinction between "study" and "books" as objects of our fondness. We need both "leisure" and "opportunity" to develop our "tastes," itself another very good term that guides what we read and hear and, indeed, play.

This marvelous freedom was well appreciated by Baring. "A boy can spend hours in the school library reading *Monte Cristo* if he wants to. Nobody cares. But supposing everyone cared and thought it a disgrace not to like Pindar, nobody would be allowed to read *Monte Cristo* or Sherlock Holmes. The tyranny of the intellect is the worst of all. The rule of the intellectuals is far severer than that of the athletes" (23). Such reflections, drawn from the library and playing fields of Eton, are well worth our intense reflection. One forgets that one of the real dangers of what are called "good schools" is the danger of leaving no time to their students for the important things, among which, no doubt, are *Monte Cristo* and Sherlock Holmes.

The accusation was often made, Baring recalls, that classical education in Latin and Greek at Eton was "useless." People proposed instead "shorthand," "book-keeping by double entry," "how to mend a motor bicycle," and "business Chinese." But Baring recalls that his "classical education was actually tempered with Mathematics, Science, French and Classical French." Thus, "it is a mistake to say we learnt nothing." Then, to prove his point, Baring proceeds to list a whole page of absolutely useless facts that are really quite amusing.

For example, consider these "facts": 1) "Troy was captured in 1184 b.c., and King Magnus was drowned in 1184 A.d." 2) "A diamond is really only a piece of charcoal." 3) "The French word *canette* means a teal as well as a flagon, and the spool in a shuttle." And, my favorite, "If you had a bamboo house and the pressure of air were taken away from it the house would swell, or smell – I forget which." The trouble with all this silliness is that, on reading the *Lost Lectures*, we cannot forget such incredible and practical "facts." And this, as Baring seems to imply, is what education is all about, the fascination with just anything, including the year King Magnus was drowned. My only problem with this is that, according to my reckoning, King Magnus Eriksson of Sweden was drowned in 1374, but there seems to be more than one King Magnus.

Baring recalls numerous memorable incidents in class or with the headmaster, Mr. Lyttelton, or companions. He speaks of the shrewdness of his companions who took considerable effort to distract the teachers so the students would not be asked what they knew. The feared test was to be on Wolsey. When Baring and his friends finally failed to distract the professor, the test was given. These were the questions asked: "1. Write a life of Wolsey. 2. What were the causes of Henry VIII's divorce? 3. Show what Charles V ruled over" (31). No wonder the boys wanted to get it postponed, and no wonder Baring could not forget the questions.

Baring remembers that much of the student's mandatory poetry, in whatever language, was written about "Spring" and usually include somewhere the phrases "O Zephyri" and "*rustica Flora.*" Writing and reciting such poetic gems of a Tuesday morning was "the scholastic event of the week." The tutors had first to check the versification of such opera. On checking, they could be heard to mutter to a fledgling Eton bard: "You've no more ear than a dead adder" (32). Of his own tutor, however, Baring paid the greatest of compliments: "He had the greatest quality a tutor can have, that of being in a certain degree all things to all boys" (33–34).

Baring's most famous teacher was probably Arthur Benson. On reading a book of poetry just published by Benson, Baring overheard Mr. Austen-Leigh, the lower master, say to him, "I did not know, Arthur, that you were such a sad man" (37). Benson was "the most natural and unconventionally-minded of all the masters." He was friendly "like a large St. Bernard." He explained to the students that "he was incapable of appreciating the great Classics, but would be delighted if they could, and stimulated them to read anything they enjoyed" (39). One can hardly find better advice.

Of the Provost of Eton, a priest, the Rev. John James Hornsby, Baring writes, "Then there was the Provost, remote and aloof from us, who preached such dull sermons in such faultless English, but who made such witty after-dinner speeches" (37). The type is not unknown to me. Though giving us no example of the dull sermon, Baring does recall a dinner in October, 1898, at Café Monico in Piccadilly. Present, all Etonians, were Lord Rosebery, Lord Curzon, Lord Minton, Bishop Weldon, and the future Prime Minister, Mr. A. J. Balfour. Lord Curzon was about to become Viceroy of India and Lord Minton the Governor-General of Canada. "The Provost in his speech said it had been claimed by the masters of the old school that they had unconsciously instilled (he pauses slightly) into their *unconscious* pupils all the necessary aptitudes for success in any walk of life: in statesmanship (and he looked at Lord Rosebery and Lord Curzon), and then (with a glance at Mr. A. J. Balfour), 'or in golf or in metaphysics.'" One cannot but be amused at the old masters of Eton instilling anything "unconsciously" into the mind of an "unconscious" pupil, however this is done. This passage is especially delightful when the pupil turns out to be a future Prime Minister, with a proficiency not in statesmanship, but in the gentle arts of "golf and metaphysics!" The Provost had both his wicked wit and his "flawless" English.

Baring could not see how any young man who knew such teachers and tutors, as he had at Eton, could complain he had "no aids towards self-education" (14). If the student learned nothing in this setting, it must have been the student's own "fault." This was not to deny that some masters were "just ragged." He recalls a mathematics tutor who did not last. There follows perhaps my favorite passage in all of this delightful chapter on Eton: "He (the new teacher) arrived completely innocent and believed everything the boys told him." To which Baring adds, "They told him a great deal." When I read that passage, I laughed out loud and to myself for several minutes. Suddenly I remembered why I loved this book and wanted to find it again.

And finally, to prove just how philosophic this book can be, Baring concludes, that "perhaps the most enjoyable of all moments at Eton was tea-time: winter teas after football with boiled eggs, or summer teas at Rowland's or Little Brown's (local bakeries or tea-houses), with new potatoes and asparagus, ending up with a strawberry mess" (42). I must confess this menu, except perhaps for the strawberry "mess," does not move my soul, at least on paper.

But, as anyone who knows of my reflections on "the Perfect Croissant and the Problem of Philosophic Learning" (*Logos*, Winter, 2002) will suspect, the next item does leave me ravenous, both bodily and philosophically. "The meal of meals was the hot baked buttered bun with coffee before early school at Little Brown's in the morning, if one had the strength of mind to get up in time for it. The bun was baked, not toasted, and had a huge wad of butter in it. One never had quite enough time to enjoy it properly; one always said to oneself one would come a little earlier next time. One never did. It was, therefore, an epitome of the highest felicities which this earth can offer" (42–43).

So I am sorry I was not at Eton in the last decade of the 19th Century, for the hot baked buttered bun at Little Brown's. This "never had quite enough time to enjoy it properly" is indeed the "epitome of the highest felicities which earth can offer." And I yet have a real fondness for the young tutor who "innocently" believed everything the boys told him. But even more, my mind whirls at not knowing the "great deal" that the boys "did tell him," which "great deal," alas, Maurice Baring neglected to record. But, having read of the imaginations of the boys in attendance with Baring at Eton, we have no trouble in imagining the bewilderment of the innocent tutor.

And how, finally, cleric that I am, can I ever forget the ordained Provost who, in spite of presence in Eton's lovely chapel, gave such "dull" sermons in, yea, "flawless" English, while at *Café Monico*, in Piccadilly, before Lords and Bishops, turned in such "witty after-dinner speeches?" I do wonder if Eton's library has copies of both the Reverend Provost's sermons and his after-dinner speeches. Are they are still studied for flawless English and for unrivaled wit?

This lecture on Eton, Baring tells us in his Preface, was originally published in the *London Mercury*. Having been "lost," I do hope many, as I, will find it again At least I am grateful to my friend who found it in a used book store in London. Finally, I shall long ponder these words of Baring: "The rule of intellect is far severer than that of athletes." This "lost lecture" on Eton seems almost more up-to-date a little over a century after he observed what went on there, as indeed does Nietzsche himself. The philosopher who announced that "God is dead" himself worried that the English were such an "un-philosophic" lot.

But Nietzsche did not know what the boys at Eton did from Monday morning to Saturday evening, after having learned on Sundays, from the "dull" sermons of the Provost, spoken in "flawless" English, in that lovely chapel, to turn the other cheek. "The tyranny of intellect is worst of all" – such are not the words of Nietzsche but of Maurice Baring, the English diplomat. He garnered them from his experiences as a boy about the playing fields and libraries of Eton. The "un-philosophic" Englishman here seems to have described the mind of the contemporary German philosopher better than the same German philosopher described the impact of Christianity on the games played by the boys at Eton. But the gentle laughter we see in all things that Baring saw at Eton makes us suspect that we are already seeing the truth of what the French novelist, Francois Mauriac, said of Baring's novels – that they were "penetrated by grace." Were this not so of Baring himself, how else could we explain the delight he saw in all things?

Chapter 19

On Willingly Being Deceived about Truth

Truth has become unfriendly. We "hold" these truths that no truth can exist, that all views are created equal, that life, liberty, and the pursuit of happiness are defined only by ourselves. They have no objective content. We have nothing in common except that we have nothing in common. Our civic peace exists on the supposition that no truth exists. Therefore, we are all "equal" in our common acceptance that no truth binds us. The order of our polity is the projection, outside of ourselves, of our souls.

To maintain that truth is important, even that such a thing exists, causes a dark suspicion of "fanaticism." To be sure, we may merely mean, culturally, that any bold affirmation is "one's own private truth." It cannot mean that anyone's "truth" has anything to do with anyone else's "truth." Certainly controversies about the truth of things cannot be resolved by human minds. We must always bracket "truth." Who, after all, dares say what it is? No source of authority exists outside of ourselves. Even when two people accidently agree that some proposition is "true," this agreement is not and cannot be the logical conclusion of a tight argument to which minds assent because they see the evidence. No evidence can "coerce" the mind to conclude this way or that. Hence, no one needs to see the truth of "truth" if he does not want to. To coin a phrase, everyone is "free to choose" his "truth."

Scripture had it quite wrong, of course. It is not "truth" that shall make us free, but precisely its lack, its denial, its impossibility that will free us. For nature, it is said, reveals no order, no basis upon which we might base any affirmation that this or that is true or false. Our own souls, moreover, reveal no internal order to which we are attuned. The suspicion that there is a "natural law" or natural order, indeed, is a most dangerous one. "Truth" is *not* following reason. It is a private projection presupposed to nothing but an order-less reality filled with order-less souls.

In third book of the *Republic*, Socrates remarks to Glaucon, "And isn't being deceived about the truth a bad thing, while possessing the truth is good? Or don't you think that to believe the things that are is to possess truth?" (413a). What's this? Surely Socrates had it all wrong. To be "deceived about the truth" should mean, in today's relativist terms, holding that truth *is* possible to know or achieve. The fundamental modern "truth," however, is that there is no truth. The *things that are* have no relation to any mind. To possess the "truth" is to see that our minds are the only source of intelligibility in the universe. Nothing out there is "speaking" to us.

In the classic view, by contrast, a world exists with its own order, an order it did not give itself but according to which it manifests itself to minds. Its truth is the relation of this order to mind, as Anaxagoras said, to a mind that knew it first. In the universe other minds are found. We ourselves possess them. They are open to this world and its order. With these minds, we can and want to know *what is*. We, on self-reflection, find minds with a kind of infinite thirst to know *what is,* to know what is not merely themselves.

In a world of no theoretic possibility of "truth," there can be no conversation, no grounds other than power to resolve differences or to affirm agreements. All our statements are mere declarations of what we "hold." Some like to think that we must agree on limiting our "truths" to what does not "harm" others. But why we should accept such limits is not so evident in lieu of some principle about why we should not harm, or even less what we mean by harm and to whom.

Truth, as I say, is unfriendly. Indeed, it is arrogant. It judges. It says of *what is* that it is, and of what is not, that it is not.

Certain principles, when embraced, destroy the mind. One of these is the claim that the mind can know nothing outside itself. A second concludes that what the mind knows cannot be communicated to another mind. A third insists that contradictory positions, which can be recognized even on the theoretical denial of truth, cannot resolve anything.

We must lower our sights. We do not co-exist with one another on the basis of agreement but of disagreement. We agree to disagree. This is our "truth." It makes us free to be what we are not. We are free to be our own self-makers and continuous self-re-makers. We are free to deceive ourselves about the *truth*.

Chapter 20

On What We Don't Know

A professor I once knew gave history tests in the following format: "Draw a line down the center of the page. On the left side, write what you know on the subject; on the right side, what you do *not* know." The logical temptation of such instruction is to put as many things possible on the left side and, on the right, a blank. How can someone be expected to write about what he does not know? The usual case is to write many things about what we do not know, but *think* we know. These are Socratic-sounding questions. We should not claim to know what we do not know.

Yet, something fascinating hovers about what we do not know. In general, we may not know something in order to concentrate on what takes much time. We are content, for instance, not to know the interesting geography of Antarctica in order to figure out how to make a better gym shoe or even how to save our soul. The human mind is infinite in what it can know. What usually prevents us from knowing something, besides a certain dullness, is time or proper training.

What substitutes for what I do not actively know? Generally, it is authority. With regard to most of the truths that we actually live by, we accept them on authority. This is as true in matters of daily living as it is true of faith. What, after all, is a map or a blueprint on how to put a toy together but a statement of authority about how something is? The assumption is that the authority knows. Following authority is not the same as acting blindly or in ignorance. Thus, "what we don't know" does not necessarily paralyze us. We can act on authority to find that it generally works.

On Tuesday, April 18, 1775, Samuel Johnson was at a beautiful Thames villa owned by a certain Mr. Cambridge. Johnson, once in the spacious house library, made a quick run over the books. Johnson overheard Sir Joshua Reynolds, in a loud "aside," criticize him "for looking only at the backs of the books." Johnson, as Boswell put it, "ever ready for contest, instantly started from his reverie, wheeled about, and answered, 'Sir, the reason is very plain. Knowledge is of two kinds. We know a subject ourselves or we know where we can find information about it. When we inquire into any subject, the first thing we have to do is to know what books have treated of it. This leads us to look at catalogues, and the backs of books in libraries'" (I, 595). Even if we do not know something, we know where to go to find it. This is a precious intelligence. Writing down what we do not know on the right hand side of the exam may have a point after all!

To translate this examining "backs of books" into modern terms, someone recently asked me about "the Illuminati," about whom I knew little. I went to Google, typed in "Illuminati, Catholic Encyclopedia." Immediately I found an essay on the topic. The Illuminati were a secret 18th society founded by a graduate of a Jesuit college. It figures.

During Christmas, visiting a nephew, I found an elegant edition of *Treasure Island*. If I read it, I no longer well recall it. I was charmed by it. The sailors on the *Hispaniola*, I read, were given "duff every other day." I wondered what this phrase meant. I do recall the colloquial expression "get off your duff." I remember asking my niece what it might mean. Maybe it meant that the sailors were given light duty every other day. But "getting off one's duff" usually meant work.

For Christmas, I was once given the *Merriam-Webster's Collegiate Dictionary*, 10th Edition. When I returned, I went to the "backs of my reference books" to this dictionary. The second meaning of "duff" is indeed "buttocks." The expression "get off your…" is given as an example. The third meaning is something "worthless" – a British expression from around 1889.

The first meaning of "duff," however, was from 1816, an alternate to "dough." It means "a boiled or steamed pudding, often containing dried fruit." A second meaning was "partly decayed matter on a forest floor." A third meaning was "fine coal." When the sailors were given "duff" every other day, it simply meant that they were given pudding! My mind was at rest.

All of this proves Johnson's point about the vastness of what we don't know. We are curious beings. We can look at the "backs of books" until we find one that is likely to inform us. What we don't know is the beginning of an adventure to take us to what we do know.

Chapter 21

What Belongs to the Wise Man

Book One, Chapter 1 of Aquinas's *Summa Contra Gentiles,* concerning wisdom, begins by citing Proverbs: "My mouth shall meditate truth, and my lips shall hate iniquity" (8:7). Aquinas finds two sides to this statement. The first is "to meditate and speak forth of the divine truth which is truth in person," the second "to refute the opposing error or impiety." Impiety is "falsehood against the divine truth." The divine truth is the "Word."

Meanwhile, in Leo Strauss's 1964 book, *The City and Man,* we find a related passage: "In the words of Thomas Aquinas, reason informed by faith, not natural reason simply, to say nothing of corrupted reason, teaches that God is to be loved and worshiped. Natural reason cannot decide which of the various forms of the divine worship is the true one, although it is able to show the falsity of those which are plainly immoral" (34). Behind Strauss's comment is the notion that the God of Aristotle had no personal relation with human beings in the world.

But which form of worship is "the true one?" Reason can at least indicate what forms are immoral. Reason should "refute the opposing error." It takes reason informed by faith, however, to tell us how God is to be worshiped and loved. Reason by itself does not inform us how God is to be worshiped. The latter is God's work. But if God has indicated how He is to be worshiped, our reason can tell us that it is not contradictory to participate in it. In doing so, it becomes more "reason."

Benedict XVI touched on this point in *Deus Caritas Est.* For the Christian, God chooses whether and what He creates. He "loves man." In contrast, "the divine power that Aristotle... sought to grasp through reflection is indeed for every being an object of desire and of love – and as the object of love this divinity moves the world – but in itself it lacks nothing and does not love: it is solely the object of love" (#9). Thus, man does worship and love God, but God first loves man. Within the Godhead exists an inner Trinitarian life. The world need not exist. If the world does exist, God can explain the world to us, including how we are to worship.

Aquinas begins the *Contra Gentiles* by telling us that the philosopher is to "name" things. The wise man is the one who sees "the order of things" and rules accordingly. We know the order from its end. The "absolutely wise man" looks to the "end of the universe." He is concerned with its "highest causes."

Aquinas next says that "the first author and mover of the universe is intellect." He adds that "the ultimate end of the universe must, therefore be, the good of the intellect." And the good of the intellect is "truth." Thus, "truth must be the ultimate end of the whole universe." These are remarkable sentences.

Aquinas continues: "Wisdom testifies that He has assumed flesh and came into the world in order to make this truth known." Aquinas understands that Aristotle does not know of this Incarnation. Yet Aquinas says, none the less, "the Philosopher (Aristotle) himself establishes that first philosophy (metaphysics) is the science of truth, not of any truth, but of that truth which is the origin of all truth, namely, which belongs to the first principle whereby all things are."

Knowledge of truth includes knowledge of what is not true. Aquinas uses the example of medicine. It "seeks to effect health and to eliminate illness." The wise medical man teaches how to effect health in the patient; this is his end. To accomplish this he must know what sickness is. Consequently, the wise man has to show what is true and refute what is false.

It is the function of the wise man to order things. The ultimate order of things betrays intellect, to the very truth of which we are to order ourselves. Only in this way are we wise.

Chapter 23

Beatrice

Two years before he died in 1945, Charles Williams, the English novelist, wrote a study of Dante called *The Figure of Beatrice*. It is simply a lovely book. This book is one I come back to every once in a while. When I do, I always stand amazed by it. It sits peacefully on my shelves. Each time I see it, even if I do not read it again, I know from the last reading that it contains the fundamental things. It is a book whose very existence is a reminder to ask oneself, often, "what is it all about, anyhow?"

The book begins by citing the *Paradiso*, xxiii, 46, in Italian – "*Riguarda qual son io.*" Roughly, this means "look at what I am." "Look!" is a command, almost as if Dante did not himself get the point of the whole *Commedia*, of his whole journey. In context, Beatrice speaks quite forcefully. The Mark Musa version (Penguin) translates this passage as follows: "Open your eyes, look straight into my face!" Looking into another's face, of course, is the essence of our longing, even for God, to see, as St. Paul said, "face to face." Implicit in "looking at what I am" is also, the "behold, *I am*." The one who gazes at me did not create me. The days of Dante's life, presumably, would have been perfectly peaceful had he not, once on a street in Florence, actually seen a real Beatrice. Thus in Paradise, on encountering her, looking at her, she wants him to know that *she is*. Look at me!

"The young," Williams writes, "are subject to a 'stupor' or astonishment of the mind which falls on them at the awareness of great and wonderful things." It is not only the young who are so struck. Again, it is not merely being "aware" that great and wonderful things exist, but realizing that such wonderful things *are* at all, that they stand outside of nothingness and we had *nothing* to do with their reality. And this awe is particularly true, as Dante understood, when what he sees is precisely a Beatrice.

Williams thinks that this experience of being "struck" by a beautiful person is not rare, but rather ordinary, as if to remind us that ordinary people also reach the highest things even by living in normal streets in Florence. None the less, the "figure" of Beatrice, that is, what we have in us caused by the reality of Beatrice, even if she is seen only once, begins to take on further levels of reality.

Williams is careful not to make Beatrice simply a product of imagination. "The subjective recollection within him (Dante) was of something objectively outside him; it was an image of an exterior fact and not of an interior desire" (7). Even though we have the power of desire, fact comes before it. Almost the whole battle with modern epistemology is contained in this one observation. What is important is not that we know, nor is it our "image" of what we know, however useful that may be. No, what is important is that which we know. Our "image" of Beatrice is ours; but what is important is not our image, but Beatrice herself. We are not Lockeans who "know" the image but not Beatrice. "The outer exterior was understood to be an image of things beyond itself."

Williams recalls in theological tradition that there are two ways to God. One is the *via negativa*, the way of "rejection." The other is the positive way, the *via affirmativa*. The *via negativa* realizes, with Dionysus, that God is beyond all our concepts, all the reality we know. When we have granted all we can to what we know, to the *what is* that we affirm, still God is beyond this affirmation. We do not, in this life, see God "face to face." To know God as *He is* we would have to be God. This we are not. If we know God *as He is* it is because He grants us the power to do so, even as we long to do so.

The negative way was probably first. "It was necessary first to establish the awful difference between God and the world before we could be permitted to see the awful likeness" (9). Dante's way, however, is a positive way. "The record of the Dantean Way begins with three things – an experience, the environment of that experience, and the means of understanding and expressing that experience; say – a woman, a city, and intellect or poetry; say again – Beatrice, Florence, and Virgil" (11). Williams has a brief and delicate discussion of the relation of such experience to marriage and the new depth to romance that revelation now makes possible. He is alert to the difference between Virgil and Dante by comparing what happened to Dido and to Beatrice.

> Dido had been the enemy of Rome, and morality had carried the hero away from Dido to Rome. But in Dante they are reconciled...

After Virgil the intellect had had visions which it communicated to the heart, if indeed they are so far separate. Since Dante the corrupt following of his way has spoiled the repute of the vision. But the vision has remained. People still fall in love, and fall in love as Dante did. It is not unusual to find them doing so (15).

What are these "visions" that follow Virgil, that the intellect "communicates" to the heart?"

This is the *via affirmativa*. This is revelation, the way to the "inGodding of man" that the Incarnation makes possible. "The way of romantic love (is) a particular mode of this same progress." Williams adds: "The general maxim of the whole way in Dante is *attention*; 'look', 'look well'. At the beginning he is compelled to look by the shock of the vision; later his attention is enforced by command and he obeys by choice. At the beginning, two of the three images – poetry and the city – are habitual to him though still fresh and young; they do not astonish him. But Beatrice does" (16).

The *via negativa* no less than the *via affirmativa* both lead beyond themselves. Beatrice's command – *"riguarda qualsonio"* – is obeyed "by choice." This voluntary mutuality is the great mystery that Chesterton touched on in his essay "In Defense of Rash Vows," the desire of all genuine lovers freely to bind themselves (*The Defendant*).

But Dante and Beatrice are not Tristan and Isolde. The *via affirmative* does not lead to love's death or denial of the world, but to its transcendence even within what it is, to its realization that it participates in the love that moves the stars. In its very perfection, there is longing. This is the *via affirmativa*. "The maxim of his (Dante's) study," Williams writes, "as regards the final Power, was: 'This also is Thou; neither is this Thou'" (8). Such words recall Augustine on the beauty of beautiful things. *"Riguarda qual son io."*

Chapter 23

Fanaticism

Browsing the other day on Internet to see if I could fi a copy of Tolstoy's *Tales Men Live By*, which someone had recommended to me, I chanced across an essay of Chesterton about Tolstoy. It is found in the Library of the University of Virginia. I had never seen it before.

Chesterton curiously begins by telling us that the best way to understand Count Leo Tolstoy was not through his novels or his ethical views, but by observing the conduct of a Russian anarchist sect in Canada called the Doukhabors. Tolstoy, it seems, had written a famous philosophic defense of their practices. In consequence of the logic of this defense, they had let their domestic animals loose "on the ground that it is immoral to possess them or control them."

What struck Chesterton about this strange act of "liberating" one's domestic animals was its rigid faith. This Russian anarchist faith is as fierce and practical as that of the Mahometans, who swept across Africa and Europe, shouting a single word. This single word was, no doubt, "Allah."

It would take a fairy-tale to "imagine the Doukhabor solemnly escorting a hen to the door of the yard and bidding it a benevolent farewell as it sets out on its travels." We can suspect that the traveling hen, suddenly out of human captivity, was soon caught and consumed by some wandering fox or wild dog. But at least, as some think, it was emancipated from immoral human beings.

Most people will think such actions as the philosophic freeing domestic animals to be merely loony. And yet this singular carrying out of what is taken to be a noble action taken in the name of liberty provides a kind of delight. "For there is only one happiness possible or conceivable under the sun, and that is enthusiasm – that strange and splendid word that has passed through so many vicissitudes, which meant, in the eighteenth century, the condition of a lunatic, and in ancient Greece, the presence of a god."

Josef Pieper, in his *Enthusiasm and the Divine Madness*, sees this word, enthusiasm, in the Platonic sense of having our world open to more than nature or our own constructions. It meant the possibility that we can be visited by the gods. Ronald Knox, in his famous book, *Enthusiasm*, saw this word to apply to movements that went beyond the normal, something that could undermine any social or religious order.

Chesterton, for his part, sees this freeing of one's animals to be an act of utter logical consistency, the meticulous carrying out of a principle. And this strict carrying out of a principle is not what is right about the act but what is wrong about it. Tolstoy has a "real, solid, and serious view of life." He is his own church. He has a view of everything flowing from his first principle.

Tolstoy's basic principle, that he applies to all else, is that of the "simplification of life." This principle governs everything we do. If something is simpler, it is better, so it is said. "When we deal with a body of opinion like this, we are dealing with an incident in the history of Europe infinitely more important than the appearance of Napoleon Bonaparte." This position is not to denigrate the importance of Napoleon but to stress the importance of what we hold. Ideas are often more important than men, even when men and personality are important.

Already for a half century before his time, Chesterton noted something that is very common today, namely the view that religion is the origin of "fanaticism." There is a whole literature today whose thesis is that religion causes "fanaticism." Indeed, this is the major issue of our time, so that the taming or eliminating of religion is the way to peace. The irony of this view is, however, that getting rid of religion will not get rid of fanaticism. Scientists and politicians, Chesterton thought, are just as capable of being "fanatics" as priests, perhaps more so. The current exclusive association of religion with fanaticism obscures its relation to science and politics.

The case of Tolstoy and the Doukhabors seems typical. "A sect of men start with no theology at all, but with the simple doctrine that we ought to love our neighbor and use no force against him, and they end in thinking it wicked to carry a leather handbag, or to ride in a (horse-driven) cart." What concerns Chesterton is the logic at work once certain first principles are embraced. There is nothing wrong with first principles or first things, of course, provided that they are really first and we deduce things properly from them.

Of Tolstoy, Chesterton continues, "A great modern writer who eras-
es theology altogether, denies the validity of the Scriptures and the
Churches alike, forms a purely ethical theory that love should be the
instrument of reform, and ends by maintaining that we have no right to
strike a man if he is torturing a child before our eyes." This same mode
of reasoning, needless to say, is behind dogmatic pacifism. Tolstoy evidently went on to hold that sex is not only immoral but also not even
natural. His logic and purity ended up in eliminating the very existence
of the body as a good, the Manichean position.

"Fanaticism has nothing at all to do with religion," Chesterton
affirms. The origins of fanaticism lie elsewhere and neither science nor
politics nor academia is immune from it. Tolstoy was no doubt a genius.
He had great faith. He lacked only one thing. "He is not a mystic and
therefore he has a tendency to go mad."

This passage recalls Chesterton's discussion of the maniac in
Orthodoxy. The maniac is not a man with many ideas that tend to bal-
ance each other off in common sense. Rather he is a man with one idea
according to which he sees all else in a distorted light. Tolstoy "is not a
mystic; and therefore he has a tendency to go mad. Men talk of the
extravagances and frenzies that have been produced by mysticism; they
are a mere drop in the bucket. In the main, and from the beginning of
time, mysticism has kept men sane." It is the mystic who is open to all
things, even if they seem at first not to make sense.

This passage on mysticism and logic is of great importance from
another angle. Chesterton in his analysis of Aquinas showed a great
interest in the variety of ordinary things, in their almost infinite capacity to arouse us to think of *what is*. He chastised the Augustinians and
the Platonists for their withdrawal from things to contemplate the One
as if they could not also find the One through particular things which
after all originated in the same One.

Chesterton comes to his main point. "The thing that has driven
them mad was logic." The poets were less likely to go insane than the
scientists – the "mad scientist" is a well-known character, in fact.
Tolstoy was deficient in poetry. "The only thing that kept the race of
men from the mad extremes of the convent and the pirate-galley, the
night-club and the lethal chamber, has been mysticism – the belief that
logic is misleading, and that things are not what they seem."

In its own way, this is an amazing passage for anyone who might
think that Chesterton was a mere rationalist. He was in fact a Thomist.

That is, he held that logic will not save us. This limitation of logic was found in Gilson's great thesis, in his *Unity of Philosophic Experience*, in his analysis of Abelard. God could not be reached by logic alone, however useful and valid logic might be in its own order.

Today, we often hear it said that "fanaticism" is the consequence of religion, that science is its alternative. If I understand Chesterton's view of both the scientists and Islam, it is that "fanaticism" stems from both. But it comes not from the original mystical insight but rather from the "logic" that flows from it that subsumes all else in its wake. Scientism denies any place for revelation in its "logic." Islam's "logic" ends up denying secondary causes or an understanding of the divinity in which diversity in the Godhead and the Incarnation is impossible. The subduing of the world to Allah is a conclusion not of the mystical insight but of the logic that follows from it.

In the end, "fanaticism" is not a product of mysticism, but of logic. By looking for its causes in the wrong place, we often reveal our own "fanaticisms." The "fanatical" concern about the religious cause of "fanaticism" has blinded us to the "fanaticisms" that stem from science itself and has caused us to misunderstand what it is within Islam that often makes it so "fanatical."

The mad man who sets his chickens loose on the grounds that it is immoral to eat them is the maniac with one idea. The cultured purist who won't even say "merry Christmas" because it violates his logic of diversity or separation of church and state is a fanatic.

Common sense does not eschew logic as such. But it does see that at the origin of things is a reality whose ways are not our ways. This is what the mystic also sees. It is the fanatic who does not see this limitation, but chooses rather to follow the logic of his position even when it leads him to absurdity. Things are, and we can know them. But likewise things "are not what they seem." We did not create them and must be prepared to find in them more than we could imagine. Call this mysticism or true philosophy or revelation, it is what we discover when we encounter *any thing that is*.

Chapter 24

What Gifts Are These?

Some months ago, I read an essay of the English Dominican, Vincent McNabb (1868–1943). In it, McNabb recalled his own family, his parents with eleven children, their Christmas in Ireland. The children received few gifts for Christmas. But, he thought, each of his brothers and sisters was a gift. A gift, after all, is a symbol of the giver. It is better to have what is given. If one has many brothers and sisters, McNabb reflected, he does not need to be inundated with toys at Christmastime. In a real sense, he observed, brothers and sisters were the real "toys," the real gifts. Their being around was more adventuresome than with any mere toy. They were such a source of life and variety that one really did not need much else. Nothing is quite as interesting as one's own brothers and sisters.

Such is a highly contentious doctrine, which, I hope, never is repeated to the population controllers who have gone a long way in depriving our kind of brothers and sisters, probably the greatest cultural loss that any civilization can know. A world of only single-child families strikes me as the definition of civilizational loneliness. A world of no brothers and sisters is a world also of no aunts and uncles, no cousins, no great-aunts and great-uncles, only parents and grand-parents. It is a world in which one's own father and mother likewise did not have brothers and sisters. The Chinese, I believe, following a "one-child policy," a hair-brained idea if there ever was one, even made it a crime to have brothers and sisters. They proceeded to destroy any brother or sister that appeared – so much for *fraternité*.

One might object, of course, that Christ was Himself an "only" child, an exception that proves the rule – an "only-begotten" Son cannot be begotten twice, it seems. In general, there are two kinds of "only" children among our kind – those from normal marital relationships in which only one child is given and those in which only one child, to put it delicately, is "permitted" by the parent or parents.

But my real topic here is not the size of families. Family size is, nevertheless, a question of ever pressing importance as societies continue to grow, as the labor pool declines, and as large numbers of foreign children arrive to replace the lost brothers and sisters and, in radical ways, change the culture.

In his famous poem, "The Cultivation of Christmas Trees," T. S. Eliot spoke of a child's "amazement at his first-observed Christmas tree." This was written before we had artificial trees, of course, though they too can be quite astonishing. I recall once being in Würzburg in Germany at Christmas. The family there followed the German custom – always so unsettling to safety-conscious Americans – of having live, burning candles on the freshly cut Tannenbaum. I remember, though considerably beyond childhood at the time, being quite amazed at that sight of the Christmas tree with lighted, not artificial, candles dancing on it. It reminded me of a much forgotten principle – if one knows how to do something, it is not dangerous. I think of this principle with regard to guns or shaving with a straight razor. But it also applies to the German Christmas trees with their flickering candles attached to the boughs of fir trees.

"What gifts are these?" I have asked. "Whose Child is this?" the Christmas hymn sings. At Christmas, I almost always come back to the notion that world itself, and all that is in it, including ourselves, is a gift. We simply are not the cause of our own being and cannot help but wonder what is. The world is not ultimately a product of "necessity," even though there are necessary things in creation, once they exist. But the world does not explain itself, even less do we explain ourselves. If anyone gives an account of his existence, after noting his parentage and place and date of birth, he soon comes to the realization that he can find no account of "why do I exist?" Our parents are just as surprised as we are by what they beget, probably more so.

The word "gift" means that something is freely presented to us that we cannot "demand." It means that what is given need not be given. But for these very reasons, it implies something quite beyond us, almost as if to tell us that we have no real idea what is given to us, even in the giving to us of ourselves. The central truth of our faith is that a Child is "given" to us. The fact of the givenness suggests an abundance beyond anything we might ourselves conceive. Once we understand this, like the child at first seeing the Christmas tree, we too can be properly amazed.

Chapter 25

"The Simplest Truth about Man"

Shortly before his untimely death, I was talking with Timothy O'Donnell, the President of Christendom College. He remarked that, in a course he once taught at Loyola-Marymount University, he always included Chesterton's *Everlasting Man*. It so happens that I have been rereading this incisive book. It is, among other things, an examination of the modern scientific mind. This is the mind that seems to have converted Chesterton to an intellectual appreciation of Catholicism. How could something be so wrong that its enemies would use arguments that contradicted each other just to make a point against it?

In *The Everlasting Man*, Chesterton broaches the question of whether man is a purely natural being who just seems to have appeared through the workings of chance and deterministic forces. Whatever actual evidence there may be for such a theory of human origins, and there is very little of it, Chesterton concludes something very striking about mankind. "The simplest truth about man is that he is a very strange being; almost in the sense of being a stranger on earth." In what, we might wonder, does this "strangeness" consist?

Chesterton's list of our strangenesses is amusing. He cannot, like some of the animals, for instance, "sleep in his own skin." He has "miraculous hands and fingers." Aristotle says that man is the only being in the universe with "hands and a mind." What is miraculous about the hand and fingers is that they can put into effect something we think up with our minds. Moreover, man "is wrapped in artificial bandages called clothes," propped up on "artificial crutches called furniture." Surely, this is odd.

But that is not all. Man's mind has incredible powers, yet it seems to be limited. "Alone among the animals, he is shaken with the beautiful madness called laughter, as if he had caught sight of some secret in the very shape of the universe hidden from the universe itself." That is a remarkable phrase – *something in the very shape of the universe hidden from the universe itself*. What could this mean? At a minimum, it means that the universe does not see or hear itself, by itself. The universe, as it were, does not know that it is a universe, that it is a whole.

But there is evidently something even more hidden than the universe's not knowing that it is itself a universe, a whole. What is that? Remember we are examining Chesterton's notion of the strangeness of our being within what is supposedly our natural environment. Man alone is "shaken" with what Chesterton happily calls "a beautiful madness." The word, "madness," of course, recalls the title of Pieper's book on Plato's *Phaedrus*, *Enthusiasm and the Divine Madness*. Here "madness" is the translation of the Greek word, *en-thousiasmos*, shaken by the Gods, by the ultimate reality outside of ourselves.

These passages in Chesterton link up again with the theme we find at the end of *Orthodoxy*, namely that the one thing that Christ has hidden from us during his life on earth was His "mirth," his joy and laughter. Chesterton proposed as the possible reason for this hiddenness was that we could not yet bear its glory. We are left in anticipation of blessedness, of beatitude. Thus, when we find Chesterton telling us in *The Everlasting Man* that man is a being "shaken" with "a beautiful madness" called precisely "laugher," we cannot help but sit up and take notice of the meaning of this "strangeness" that distinguishes us from all other beings. Evidently, it may not distinguish us from the Gods, but indicate something we have in common with them.

Chesterton continues with his withering critique of so much science. "It is not natural to see man as a natural product. It is not common sense to call man a common object of the country or the seashore. It is not seeing straight to see him as an animal. It is not sane. It sins against the light; against that broad daylight of proportion which is the principle of all reality." What have we here? If it is not natural to see man as natural, how is it a sin "against that broad daylight of proportion which is the principle of all reality" to find him to be a stranger in the same universe?

Chesterton, of course, implies that man's "proportion" within all reality is that he is the sole being in the universe directly made for God in each of his personal appearances within time. The proportion is restored, as Plato also implied, when this same man looks out on the strangeness of the said universe and his own place within it to suspect, because he laughs, that the mystery behind the universe is by no means dull or joyless. It is full of the "madness" that takes us out of ourselves when we think the only thing we need to know about the world is what in fact we know about it by our own powers.

Later on in *The Everlasting Man*, Chesterton talks of something called "the Religion of Humanity." Such a rationalistic religion, evidently, worships "corporate mankind as a Supreme Being." The alternative to the Trinitarian God of revelation is an abstract collectivity composed of all mankind, probably only those living, as rationalists usually do not hold the immortality of the soul. Just how this collectivity is imagined to be the "Supreme Being" is somewhat mind-boggling.

But, to return to our theme of laughter at the heart of things, Chesterton examines the premise of the collectivity as the Supreme Being on the basis of the logic of proportion. In other words, he takes the rationalists at their word and finds them delightfully funny. "Even in the days of my youth, I remarked that there was something slightly odd about despising and dismissing the doctrine of the Trinity as a mystical and even maniacal contradiction; and then asking us to adore a deity who is hundred million persons in one God, neither confounding the persons nor dividing the substance." Thus, the strangeness of the strangest being lies in the fact that he can see the oddness in explanations of the Supreme Being that miss the point of what He is. The simplest truth about man is that he is a very strange being. This "beautiful madness" that we call "laughter" somehow reaches the oddest thing about us. The universe does not know itself. We are the beings in the universe who know it. And once we know this, we have a choice. We have to decide whether this universe is a gift to us, including ourselves as somehow the strangest beings in it, or whether it has nothing to say to us except the negative admonition, "do what you want." The first path, I suspect, leads to joy, the second to despair. This too is a simple truth about man.

Chapter 26

The Young Tyrant

A recurring theme in Plato's dialogues, including his Seventh Letter, describes the education of a young man who wants to achieve the highest things, which he considers to be achieved primarily by his own ruling the polity. He wants to be a tyrant. This desire, he explains to others, means that he wants to "do good" and thereby receive high honors. The young man's father or brother brings him to Athens to ask if Socrates might take the young man under his wing to prepare him for this worthy task.

Often, the young man is rich and quite handsome, though, in the case of Theages, he is sickly. This illness is what prevented him from achieving his goal, to his good fortune, as it turns out. Socrates, unlike most college professors, does not take a fee. Socrates is sometimes offered emoluments, but this is what the Sophists receive. Socrates thus must first be "persuaded" or "convinced" that the young man is worth the effort. Socrates teaches that before a man can rule others, he has to rule himself, no mean feat.

The Sophists, perhaps unkindly, are considered the first college professors. They teach how to rule through eloquence alone. Socrates did not like Sophists. They were often quite famous celebrities. When they came to town, the potential philosophers, the aspiring youth of Athens, the sons of the existing rulers, turned out to hear them.

The city's best entertainment occurs when Socrates is provoked to debate these visiting dignitaries. The plot of many dialogues concerns the education of a young man who wants to rule but who has no idea what this ruling involves, especially in himself. Socrates does not see too much hope for most of them, though sometimes he gives it a try. They have already all they want to rule.

The souls of the young men are already formed by their desires for fame, pleasure, or wealth. All you can do is save others from them. The first line of a city's liberty begins here, in the souls of its best. Plato says, ominously, in his Seventh Letter: "We know that the requests of tyrants are mingled with compulsion" (329d). The great tyrants arise in democracies, the Republic tells us. Those who want to rule are charming, handsome, and eloquent.

Of all these young men, Alcibiades was the most attractive and the most dangerous. In Alcibiades I, we read:

> Socrates: "So it's not walls or war-ships or shipyards that cities need, Alcibiades, if they are to prosper, nor is it numbers or size, without virtue." Alcibiades: "Definitely." Socrates: "So if you are to manage the city's business properly and well, you impart virtue to the citizens." Alcibiades: "Of course." Socrates: "Is it possible to impart something you haven't got?" Alcibiades: "How could it be?"..... Socrates: "So what you need to get for yourself and for the city isn't political power, nor the authority to do what you like, what you need is justice and self-control.... When an individual or a city with no intelligence is at liberty to do what he or it wants, what do you think the likely result will be?" (137b–e)

We need some experience of polities to know what this result might be.

Demodocus brings his son, Theages, to Socrates because the young man apparently wants to be wise. Socrates chats with the youth. Yes, he discovers, Theages wants to be wise. On examination, this being wise means that he wants to be like Hippias and Periander. They are the great and most corrupt tyrants of Greek experience, as everyone knows. Socrates is astounded at the young man's choice.

"You rascal! So you want to be a tyrant over us, and that's why you criticized your father all along for refusing to send you to some tyrant-teacher" (124e–25a). On pressing the young man about the awful way these famous tyrants ruled, Theages backtracks. No, he does not want to imitate the "violence" of their rule. Rather, "I want to rule over those who voluntarily submit" (126a). The kid sounds like he read Rousseau!

It turns out, though, that to rule over willing citizens, one must first become wise. He needs a teacher to teach him not about politics but about wisdom. Of course, the only way to learn such wisdom is to associate with Socrates.

Indeed, we might say that the first step in politics is to test one's soul against the important things which are not political. Tyrants, intelligent, charming men as they usually are, rush into politics without first examining their souls. Politics without wisdom is not politics.

We know that the requests of tyrants are mingled with compulsion.

The Greek meaning of democracy is the rule of those for whom freedom as whatever it is that they want it to mean. The Greek meaning of tyranny comes forth when the Greek meaning of democracy rules. The tyrant orders everything, including the polity, to himself and his wants.

The modern experience of tyranny follows the idealism with repression that Plato described. The modern notion of democracy becomes in practice the ancient notion of tyranny.

At the end of the *Gorgias*, Socrates says: "I believe that I am one of the few Athenians… to take up the true political craft and practice the true politics" (521d). He could say that because he knew that his soul was made for something other than politics.

Chapter 27

The Infinite Anguish of Free Souls

In Albert Camus's *Lyrical and Critical Essays*, (Vintage, 1968), I found a 1940 essay entitled, "The Almond Trees." This collection has long been a favorite of mine. It bears much of the somberness of the then upcoming War. Camus himself was from Algeria. "When I lived in Algiers, I would wait patiently all winter because I knew that in the course of one night, one cold, pure February night, the almond trees of the Vallée des Consuls would be covered with white flowers." But the blossoms, though sturdy, were brief. Camus adds, "There is no symbol here." He does not refer to the passingness of things, either of empires or of lives.

Camus has a third reflection, a remarkable one, "We will not win our happiness with symbols." With what, we might ask, are we then to "win" our happiness, if indeed it is something to be won? I am glad that neither our happiness nor our lives are merely symbols, though I have heard of philosophers who speak of "real symbols." If, indeed, we are all "made flesh" in a *word*, as I suspect we are, then we might well be called "real symbols," and our real happiness is "symbolic" precisely because it is not mere symbol, a mere word without flesh.

Camus began this essay soberly. As he noted in his 1939 journal, he had read a passage from Napoleon in which the great Emperor had compared power and mind. Napoleon thought, perhaps contrary to Machiavelli, that mind would always "conquer the sword." I say of Machiavelli "perhaps" because he himself remained "an unarmed prophet." He too sought to conquer minds.

Camus reflected that during the previous wars of Europe, it was often not the conqueror who became famous, but the mystic, the artist, or the writer who recorded what the war and the time meant. "The Hundred Years War has likewise been forgotten, and yet the prayers of Silesian mystics still linger in some hearts." Camus thought that because the monk and the painter were drafted into modern armies, there was no longer this distinction between war and thought which even a Napoleon could respect. Camus added the following rather prophetic comment: The mind today "exhausts itself in cursing force, for want of knowing how to master it." In other words, the crisis is not so much in military power as in the minds of the dons, the monks, the artists.

In any case, many deplore this result, this confusion. They say "it is evil." But Camus, reminding one of a passage from *The Apology*, observes, "We do not know if it is evil, but we know it is a fact." Socrates had replied that he did not know whether death was an evil. All he knows is that "to do wrong was evil."

Camus next adds the following comment: If we do not know whether the mind is not evil or whether it can win over power, we still must act. We must be what were once called, like Camus himself, existentialists. They proposed that we act even if we did not have in our minds a structure of the world, with its distinction of good and evil, in which to act. "All we need to know, then, is what we want. And what we want precisely is never again to bow beneath the sword, never again to count force as being in the right unless it is serving the mind." But of course there are philosophers, men of the mind, who themselves are corrupt. Camus's action can never avoid the question of the right ordering of being.

Camus is not a rationalist. "I do not have enough faith in reason to subscribe to a belief in progress or any philosophy of history." Whatever we might think of the old-fashioned theory of progress, itself a sort of secularization of salvation history, it is clear that we must have enough "faith in reason" to reject the notion, which has subsequently surfaced with such force, that there is no order, nothing but will, as both Machiavelli and Nietzsche thought.

Camus continues with his effort to be unreasonably reasonable. "We know that we live in contradiction, but we know that we must refuse this contradiction and do what is needed to reduce it. Our task as men is *to find the few principles that will calm the infinite anguish of free people*." I paused for a long time when I read those lines: "a few principles that will calm the infinite anguish of a free people." I wondered if "un-free people" also had infinite anguish? Can this be done, we wonder, this calming of "infinite anguish?" Can it be done with these philosophical premises that ask us to "live in contradiction?"

Or perhaps our "infinite anguish" arises precisely because we are "free." The structure of the world may not be independent of our choices. And our choices may not bear that unlimited freedom that is not bound by the principle of contradiction. The hypothesis that our freedom cannot or does not lead to a truth – this itself may be the real problem.

Camus cautions us to "make justice imaginable" in a world of injustice. Happiness needs to be seen as possible for those who thought it hopeless. Camus adds, in words I presume he did not mean for us to take literally, though that may be the only way they make sense, "Naturally, it is a superhuman task." He evidently does not mean "supernatural," as if to say that there are answers that are of reason but also beyond our own reason initially to formulate.

Camus adds, "But superhuman is the term for tasks men take a long time to accomplish." This is a strange definition of "superhuman," that is, "what takes a long time to accomplish." Logically that would make everything mankind has ever done to be "superhuman." The answer thus is not from "beyond time"; it is only a question of "more" time. Camus is ultimately comforted by the fall of other civilizations; he thinks it is a sign of ordinariness. He thinks ours is not the last civilization, even should it fall.

"Let us not listen too much to those who proclaim that the world is at an end." The times were not apocalyptic. With this reflection, we are to be comforted. We need the "virtues of the mind." We need "strength of character." Camus reverts to the almond tree, whose blossoms are brief against the cold winds but prepare the fruit in due season. He has almost returned to the Greek notion of cyclic history.

And yet, there is "the infinite anguish of free souls." "Why infinite?" we wonder. Is it because, as Aristotle said, that no natural desire is "in vain?" Is it because we are intended to feel in our souls precisely an anguish that is "infinite" so that we ultimately, while not necessarily deprecating it, realize that action, and hence virtue, are not enough for us?

Chapter 28

"The Great Art O' Letter-Writin'"

Chapter XXXIII of *The Pickwick Papers* bears the following title: "Mr. Weller the elder delivers some critical sentiments respecting literary composition; and, assisted by his son, Samuel, pays a small installment of retaliation to the account of the reverend gentleman with the red nose." In the course of this fascinating chapter, the younger Mr. Weller is engaged in the happy task of writing a Valentine letter to "Mary, Housemaid, at. Mr. Nupkin's, Mayor's, Ipswich, Suffolk," whom he has seen but once. This Valentine was to be put into the General Post.

This particular Valentine letter, however, occasioned the presenting certain principles of letter writing that no one ought to overlook. Recently, I chanced to discuss briefly with a student from Venezuela, of all places, the influence of E-mail on the ancient tradition of letter writing. The instantaneousness of it is perplexing. The old post took time. It allowed a certain savoring, a certain rumination. By contrast, E-mail seems so ephemeral – a blip on a screen. Moreover, any E-mail letter can be forwarded to someone else or saved in some hard disc. It is difficult to know what happens to it. Unlike the letter sent by General Post, however, unless printed out, the E-mail letter exists only electronically. And there is something dramatically different between a printed out E-mail letter and a hand-written letter received in the mail.

"To ladies and gentlemen not in the habit of devoting themselves practically to the science of penmanship," we read in *The Pickwick Papers*, "writing a letter is no very easy task; it being always considered necessary in such cases for the writer to recline his head on his left arm, so as to place his eyes as nearly as possible on a level with the paper...." The very notion of "penmanship" is made unnecessary with E-mail, or even more so by talk E-mail. But one wonders just what sort of writing was possible with one's head on his left arm with eyes on the level with the paper?

The importance of this topic of writing a letter is made clearer by what follows in *The Pickwick Papers*. The elder Mr. Samuel Weller was anxious that his son Samuel did not do anything rash in writing his Valentine. It was a dangerous business.

> "I've done now," said Sam with a slight embarrassment; "I've been a writin'." "So I see," replied (the elder) Mr. Weller. "Not to any young 'ooman, I hope, Sammy?" "Why, it's no use a sayin' it ain't," replied Sam. "It's a walentine." "A what!" exclaimed Mr. Weller, apparently horror-stricken by the word. "Samuel, Samuel," said Mr. Weller, in reproachful accents, "I didn't think you'd ha' done it. Arter the warnin' you've had o' your father's wicious propensities...."

The elder Mr. Weller was worried that Sam would be married. But Sam assured him that this was not his intention, even though he was sending the Valentine to Mary, in Ipswich.

So young Sam read a bit of the letter to his father. They have some brandy to help the composition. The father warns Samuel not to write any poetry, which is "unnat'ral." The pen keeps leaking and it is necessary to blot the paper. "Go on, Sammy." He does:

> "Feel ashamed and completely circumscribed in addressin' of you, for you *are* a nice gal and nothin' but it." "That's a wery pretty sentiment," said the elder Mr. Weller, removing his pipe to make way for the remark. "Yes, I think it is rayther good," observed Sam, highly flattered. "Wot I like in that 'ere style of writin'," said the elder Mr. Weller, "is that there ain't no callin' names in it – no Weneses, or nothin' o' that kind. Wot's the good o'callin' a young 'ooman a Wenus or a angel, Sammy?" "Ah, what, indeed?" replied Sam.

Sam, Jr. clearly is not totally convinced of his father's wisdom here.

Sam, Jr. proceeds to explain in his Valentine to Mary that "'Afore I see you, I thought all women was alike." The father quite agrees with this observation. But Sam, Jr. has found his voice. He tells Mary that the first and only time he saw her his heart beat faster. On hearing this human weakness, the elder Mr. Weller replies, "I am afeerd that werges on the poetical, Sammy." Young Sam denies it. But this is how he concludes the letter to Mary, at Mr. Nupkin's. "'Except of me Mary my dear as your walentine and think over what I've said. My dear Mary, I will now conclude,' "That's all," said Sam." The elder Mr. Weller inquired, "That's rather a sudden pull up, ain't it, Sammy?" And then comes the line that I first occasioned these reflections: "'Not a bit on it,' said Sam; 'she'll vish there was more, and that's *the great art o' letter writin'*."

The great art of letter writing is that the recipient would wish for more. Of course, I must add, that the question came up between the two Wellers about signing this particular letter. Young Sam wanted to end in verses but did not want to sign his own name. The elder gentleman did not like the verses. The young Weller affirmed, "never sign a walentine with your own name." So the elder Weller suggested that he sign it "Pickwick," and he does, "Your love-sick, Pickwick." Needless to say, this solution will cause no end of confusion.

We have it all here, letter-writing and penmanship, letter writing and sentiment, letter writing and proportion. We are finite beings. It takes time to disclose ourselves. Things need time to settle, especially written things. And while something anonymous hovers about the classical Valentine, the essence of letter-writing is that it is person to person without the medium of the world except for the paper and the penmanship. Samuel Weller is right. There is an art of letter writing, a fine art, indeed.

Chapter 29

Mathematics

In his Verona address (October 19, 2006), Benedict XVI returned to a theme he had broached in his Regensburg lecture, namely, the relation between modern science, with its "mathematical" foundation, and the existing things of nature. In the Regensburg lecture, the Pope related this mathematical background to Plato and Descartes. What is at issue here might seem, at first sight, to be relatively esoteric and hardly an issue of revelation. Yet, this issue touches, in its own way, the very credibility of faith and its relation to reason.

Everyone knows that great minds in mathematics seem to burn out early. Mathematics, while being its own discipline, rooted in quantity, and hence related to things that can be measured by norms reducible to mathematics, is something we are all supposed to study early in our training. We learn mathematics before we learn philosophy, as Plato wisely taught us.

Plato also tells us that the study of mathematics and geometry is quite useful for us. We cannot make change in a grocery store without it, nor can we build fortifications that hold up. Mathematics has a certain fascination because of its clarity. We are all aware that many ethical and political problems can only be resolved "for the most part." Mathematics seems to give the mind that rare form of experience, that is, clearly established certitude. We are tempted to want all our problems to be solved with the same clarity.

No doubt, such problems could be so solved if we were all nothing but objects or products of mathematical formulae. I once heard of a scientist who proposed that we all can be formulated in terms of mathematical equations, however complicated. On this basis, it was supposed, the resurrection of the body would not be such a big problem. Secretly, I rejoice in the fact that if Schall is, in fact, a mathematical configuration, he remains, contrary to Socrates' admonition, still too dull ever to "know himself " in these terms.

The Pope, of course, had something else in mind. He wanted to acknowledge the place of mathematics both in itself and in its relation to nature. Contrary perhaps to Descartes, the Pope did not want to have to prove the existence of God before he could relate his mental idea of things to existing things themselves. "Mathematics, as such," Benedict observed, "is a creation of our intelligence: (there exists) a correspondence between its structures and the real structures of the universe." Mathematics understood as such, as a systematic, conscious exposition of itself, exists only in the mind. But there is something curious about this existence in the mind since it obviously has some relation to "real structures of the universe." The reason bridges fall down is usually because of some mathematical error in their construction. Otherwise, they stand up and we know why they stand up.

Modern science and technology, Benedict continues, "presupposes" this correspondence. He refers approvingly to Galileo's famous formula. "The book of nature is written in mathematical language." What Benedict is concerned with here, however, is what he calls the "self-limitation" of science. This "self-limitation" is designed to restrict science from talking about anything that is not mathematical in structure. Yet no mind can simply let this relationship between mathematics and really existing things just sit there unattended to in his mind. In fact, it leads to what the Pope calls "a big question."

What is this question? The relation implies that "the universe itself is structured in an intelligent manner, such that a profound correspondence exists between our subjective reason and the objective reason in nature." Many will try to avoid what comes next, but it is in the logic of the argument. It becomes "inevitable to ask oneself if there might not be a single original intelligence that is the common font of them both." Wonder thus arises about whether an order exists that includes both the mind and the world, since, however delicately, some correspondence between the two is already found in existence.

The Pope, of course, here seeks to formulate the truth found in science over against the notion that there are uses of the intelligence, other methods, that are not strictly mathematical. Not all being is quantity. He does not deny that the mathematical is itself a legitimate and welcome use in its right area.

The human mind, looking at the universe, notices that the mathematics that it formulates has a basis in the reality that this mind did not itself make. The question arises, why is there mind? Why is there universe? It is neither unreasonable nor unscientific to wonder if they have a common source that might already include the origins of both.

Chapter 30

"A Place Which I Have Never Yet Seen"

Belloc I have long considered simply the best essayist in the English language. I am quite capable of saying the same of Chesterton. In any case, Chesterton is today clearly much better known than Belloc. These two men were great friends; they talked together over much of their respective lifetimes about the highest things and about everything, even about "nothing" as Belloc wrote in a famous essay. In having both their writings we are simply blessed. The opportunity to write something rather regularly on Belloc, as I have for many years on Chesterton in the *Midwest Chesterton News*, is something to which I distinctly look forward.

I have long grown skeptical of any idea that a thing is necessarily good because it is well-known. Many well-known things are quite bad. Some of the very best things, like, say, the Nicene Creed, are not very well-known even when they are well-known and to be recited every Sunday. We cannot think of Chesterton without in some sense thinking of Belloc. I have always found each in his own way to be a source of delight, wisdom, insight, truth, and, especially in the case of Belloc, of a certain poignancy, or nostalgia, that has constantly touched my soul whenever I came across it.

The reader of this column will find me talking about this poignant side of Belloc rather a lot. Belloc was a man who walked and sailed and remembered. This is not to be a scholarly column, nor a matter of historical insight into Belloc's time and writings. I gladly leave that task to others. The good reader will find here the Belloc that moved my soul, the Belloc that brought me to places and to things and to persons I would never have otherwise met or known about. Belloc was a man of this earth in the only way a man can be a man of this earth, by being unsettled in it and by it, especially by its beauty, by the memory of things past, even by the memory of things that might have been otherwise.

My book *Idylls and Rambles: Lighter Christian Essays* (Ignatius Press, 1994) contains fi chapters. Why? Because this is the number of essays in J. B. Morton's collection *Selected Essays of Hilaire Belloc* (Methuen, 1948). This wonderful book was actually being discarded from the library of a religious house in San Francisco in which I was living at the time. I retrieved it. The house's loss is definitely my gain.

The fifty-fourth and last essay in the Morton collection is entitled "On Dropping Anchor." The essay begins, "The best noise in all the world is the rattle of the anchor chain when one comes into harbour at last and lets it go over the bows." Now, I am not sailor enough to know this rattling sound, nor why it might be the "best noise in all the world," even though my last name, in German, means "noise or sound, especially, as I like to think, the sound of a bell."

In sailing one does not always drop anchor, but rather picks up stationary moorings. This means that there is no anchor dropping. But this mooring situation is always precarious, as Belloc recounts in his trying to tie up the *Silver Star* at an empty mooring by the Royal Yacht Squadron grounds up the Medina. He had, however, tied up at a rich man's moorings. According to the custom of courtesy, Belloc recounts, one can "pick up any spare mooring one could find." The rich man, who appeared with his big yacht on the scene, did not think so. Belloc's moral reflection on this incident of the rich man denying his little boat common courtesy was memorable: "Riches, I thought then and I think still, corrupt the heart."

The next tangle with moorings happened to Belloc when he was sailing to Orford town over the bar of the Orford River. Belloc and his companion spotted a buoy and tied up to it, much to the objections of the people on shore. To his surprise, the mooring did not hold his boat. He could not figure out why until he realized that he had tied up to a temporary mooring set up for a rowing regatta, which was why the folks on shore were trying to shout at him not to tie up there. The incident so struck Belloc that he wrote an eighteen line poem about it. "The men that lived in Orford stood / Upon the shore to meet me…"

From this experience, Belloc concludes that it is better to have moorings of one's own, or else to use one's own anchor and hear the chains rattle. This situation of anchors and moorings sets Belloc to further reflection: "I love to consider a place which I have never yet seen, but which I shall reach at last, full of repose and marking the end of those voyages, and security from the tumble of the sea." No wonder Morton chose this essay for the last essay in the Collection!

Belloc then proceeds to imagine such a place that he shall "reach at last." It shall be a cove surrounded by high hills with no houses or signs of men. There should be a little beach and a "breakwater made by God." The tide shall smoothly come in and out of the cove, like a "cup of refreshment and of quiet, a cup of ending." He shall guide his boat up the fairway into the channel and on into the cove that will be cut off from an opening to the sea. The sea he shall see no more, though he can still hear its noise. All around will be silence. "All alone in such a place, I shall let go the anchor chain, and let it rattle for the last time." He will let the anchor into the clear and salty water, maybe four lengths or more, so that the boat may swing at its anchor. Once secure, he will "tie up (his) canvas and fasten all for the night and get ready for sleep."

This will be the end of Belloc's sailings, in this lovely, imaginary cove, with the steep hills surrounding, the anchor chains finally rattling into the blue, salty water. "And that will be the end of my sailing." The Belloc who sails no more, of course, is the Belloc who has finally come home into his cove, who has finished with what delights and dreams this world has given to him in his *Silver Star*.

Let me repeat again these nostalgic, memorable words: "I love to consider a place which I have never yet seen, but which I shall reach at last, full of repose and marking the end of those voyages, and security from the tumble of the sea." This is the human condition, isn't it? We live in a world that makes us love to consider a place we have not yet seen, a place that we shall reach at last. The "end" of Belloc's sailing is, after all, our end, isn't it?

Chapter 31

My Sister's Piano

My sister Norma Jean has a Baldwin Grand Piano. She acquired it when she and her husband were living in Phoenix in about 1982. It has since moved to Texas, Wisconsin, Oregon, and twice in Southern California. For ten years before Phoenix, she had a console-type piano. Before that, ever since I can remember, she had an upright piano that belonged to our mother. My mother died in 1937, when Jeannie was about six years old.

Aunt Fran, my mother's next older sister – my mother had thirteen siblings – told Jeannie that when she was younger, my mother was the only one in the large family who could play the piano. Her parents used to love to hear her play, which she did at family occasions like Christmas and family reunions. This would have been in the big farmhouse outside of Pocahontas, in Iowa.

I can vaguely remember this upright piano. My mother had taken it with her when she married our father. I was old enough to recall her playing in the house on Main Street in Knoxville, also in Iowa, not long before she died. While I am something of a klutz with regard to music, I was given piano lessons while my mother was still alive. I often have wondered, had she lived, whether I would have learned to play. But my sister Jeannie as she grew up inherited the piano. We all knew it was hers. She learned to play. One of our Schall cousins recalled Jeannie playing when she was quite young. She became better and better as the years went by. She minored in music in college at San Jose State.

When, some five years after my mother's death, my father remarried a lovely widow with two daughters my own age, I recall often that Jeannie would play in the big front room in the Washington Street house in Knoxville. She, with our new stepsister, Jeanne Louise, would sing together at Christmas and indeed often. I can still hear them laughing and singing together. Christmas to me means, in terms of memory, Jeannie playing the songs of that season on that piano that had belonged to our mother. Sounds somehow can make things more real than sight.

I recall my father sometimes singing, but never realized till now when I think about it that what he sang was probably from the piano that mother played.

When our family moved to San Jose in California in 1945, the piano was boxed and shipped with the other household goods. In a way, that piano still gives me nightmares. When the truck arrived, it backed into the narrow driveway of the McKendrie Street house. My father, brothers, some neighbors, and the truck driver came to the point of unloading the heavy piano. They used a sort of steel track on which to slide the boxed piano down to the ground from the truck. I was stationed next to the house with some bushes alongside.

As the piano came down, it began to tip off the railings in my direction. I could not hold it up. Fortunately, it fell against the bushes and house, thereby saving Schall, at an early age, from being smashed by his sister's piano. It taught me a first principle: "You can never be too careful unloading pianos." If I close my eyes, I can still see the piano tipping over my way. Every human life, I suppose, includes a near-miss or two. We call it luck or providence, not that luck does not fall under providence in a sound philosophy.

After Ordination and my early Roman time, I have been in my sister and brother-in-law's home almost every year no matter where they were. It is always something close to my being to sit quietly as my sister plays her Baldwin piano. She has collected a considerable amount of sheet music over the years. While she lived in Medford, in Oregon, she used to play in various senior citizens' homes. She would often comment on the effect of music on those good souls almost too old to remember anything; how they would light up on hearing some song that they knew.

Jeannie plays a wide variety of music – classical, church, Protestant hymns, Irish, western, Spanish, popular, from various decades. As I listen to it, her music always – how else to put it? – refreshes my soul. How very nice to have such a sister who will play for her brother! Jeannie usually knows when the song she is playing was written, by whom, who sang it, what movie or play, if any it was in. Sometimes she will also sing it, if it is sing-able.

Jeannie does much of her own arrangements, which she learned to do from a course which she once took while they were living in Simi Valley. She plays in her parish on an electronic piano. I am not much of a fan of electronic instruments. I cringe when I go into a church for

Mass to find a line of electronic guitars and keyboards waiting for me. So I am glad the Baldwin is simply a classic piano, even though her church piano sounds fine.

Over the years, I have often taught courses that include Plato, Aristotle, and Augustine, each of whom wrote a treatise on music. At first, I never took seriously what the classical writers said about music. I was somewhat puzzled by the amount of space that music took in the *Republic* and in the *Politics*. Indeed, they said that a change in music will signify a change in polity. What finally woke me up, I think, was the chapter on music in Bloom's *The Closing of the American Mind*. I have known families who send their children off to rock concerts as if they are just another "entertainment."

But Bloom too has read Plato. Music is not just another "entertainment." I often realized while listening to my sister that music does move one's soul. Listening to her play can change one's whole mood. As Aristotle says, music will reproduce in us the motions in the human voice under emotion. We are formed by what we hear, whether we know it or not. A disorder in music leads to a disorder of soul. This subtle influence is why Bloom said that the real educator of youth today is not the school or the parents but the music-makers. Robert Reilly's essays in his *Surprised by Beauty* on whether music can be sacred have also taught me much. The association of music and divinity is not merely accidental.

By now everyone has noticed that we have a pope whose brother is a Kappelmeister. Benedict himself plays Mozart on the piano just because he loves it. This ability is not a requirement for the Office, I suppose, but it surely does not hurt it. Reading between the lines, one senses that Benedict is rather annoyed by the awfulness that we too often hear in church music in recent decades. Indeed, he says as much. "Is it just a difference in taste?" we wonder. Benedict seems to think that one of the main consequences of revelation is in fact beauty, including, perhaps beginning with, beautiful music.

The notion of the "heavenly choirs" in which we will all participate is, I suppose, both profound and amusing. "You mean all you do in heaven is sit around and sing? Surely part of the answer is, "Well, yes, of course." There is probably on this earth no experience quite like singing a Hayden or Bach Oratorio in a large choir with full concert orchestra before a silent, riveted audience. Music is not an occupation but a celebration of something beyond itself. Let us hope, in any case, that the heavenly choirs are closer to Mozart than much of the raucous music we hear. Still, I think of my sister's piano. It means that any home can have its own music played by someone within it. German and Czech families will often have string quartets midst their members, at least in the days that the Germans and Czechs had children. Eric Voegelin, himself a lover of music, once remarked that no one needs to participate in the aberrations of his time. This is true of music too, something I learned listening to my sister play her Baldwin Grand Piano.

Chapter 32

On Making Atheists of Tenants

Joseph Addison (1672–1719), in his essays, follows the career of Sir Roger de Coverley. Sir Roger's well-appointed estate in the country includes a rather learned chaplain-in-residence. Addison begins his essay, "Sunday in the Country," with the following striking observation: "I am always very well pleased with a country Sunday and think, if keeping holy the seventh day were only a human institution, it would be the best method that could have been thought of for polishing and civilizing mankind." But the real problem is why in fact did not some civil institution invent it then? This thesis might be called the "side-effects" value of revelation. For not a few more contemporary folks, however, the slovenly garb and tacky music seen and heard at Sunday Mass since Vatican II do cast some doubt on the validity of this otherwise noble thesis. Some pessimists even see it as a decline of civilization.

If country people did not have the opportunity to dress up, to show their manners and refinement with others on a Sunday, Addison thinks, they would probably soon devolve into "savages and barbarians." On a country Sunday, however, what happens is this: "the whole village meet together with their best faces, and in their cleanliest habits, to converse with one another on indifferent subjects, hear their duties explained to them, and join together in adoration of the Supreme Being." This is mindful of the thesis of Dawson and Pieper that the root of culture is always religion.

This Sunday occasion puts the cares of the week aside. On this day, both sexes appear "in their most agreeable forms, and exerting all their qualities as are apt to give them a figure in the eye of the village." Conversation in the Church-yard is a place in which any "country fellow" can distinguish himself.

It seems that Sir Roger was anxious that all his tenants attended church services. Indeed, he checked on them. "As Sir Roger is landlord to the whole congregation, he keeps them in very good order, and will suffer nobody to sleep in it besides himself." If Sir Roger does nap during a sermon, "upon recovering out of it he stands up and looks about him, and if he sees anybody else nodding, either wakes them himself or sends his servants to them." He even hired an "itinerant singing-master" to teach the congregation how to sing. Sir Roger gave each of the flock a hassock on which to rest, and a Book of Common Prayer.

Addison recounts the instance of being in Sir Roger's church when a certain John Matthews, "remarkable for being an idle fellow," evidently "kicked his heels for diversion." What was Sir Roger's reaction? He called out to John Matthews "not to disturb the congregation." Now though this action of Sir Roger's seemed a bit much to any spectator, "the general good sense and worthiness of his character make his friends observe these little singularities as foils that rather set off than blemish his good qualities."

After the sermon on Sunday, no one leaves before Sir. Roger. As he departs, Sir Roger has a word with each tenant and inquires about any family member he does not see in church. This little gesture "is understood as a secret reprimand to the person that is absent." Presumably, the said absentee will be there the following Sunday.

If a young man does his catechism well, Sir Roger may give the lad a Bible or his mother a "flitch of bacon," as a reward for such hard work.

Evidently, the good fellowship that exists between Sir Roger and his chaplain is unusual. For in the very next parish, the squire and the parson "live in a perpetual state of war" – a phrase that is redolent of Hobbes himself, *bellum omnium contra omnes*. The result of this "contention" between the neighboring squire and parson has quite unfortunate results. "The parson is always preaching at the squire; and the squire, to be revenged on the parson, never comes to church."

What might we expect to be the result of this squire-parson altercation? It could not be worse. "The squire has made all his tenants atheists and tithe-stealers." Every Sunday, the parson speaks of the dignity of clergy-hood, hinting that he is "a better man than his patron." Things have come to such an "extremity" that the squire has not said public or private prayers "this half year." Confronted with this dire situation, the parson threatens to "pray" for the squire "in face of the whole congregation." I presume this latter threat means that the squire is thereby branded as a sort of public sinner.

Addison reflects on the unfortunate consequences of a dispute between squire and parson – can we say, in contemporary terms, between "church and state?" These too frequent "feuds" are "very fatal to the ordinary people, who are so used to be dazzled with riches, that they pay as much deference to the understanding of a man of an estate, as of a man of learning." It is to be recalled that Sir Roger's chaplain was probably an Oxford man.

When the squire and the parson have radically different views, the consequences are dire. Why? The answers of Addison in his reflection on the "country Sunday" are sobering. For the common folk "are very hardly brought to regard any truth, how important soever it may be, that is preached to them, when they know there are several men of five hundred a year who do not believe it." There we have it! The whole inner workings of the spirit are revealed. Here is the reason why reason and revelation must be seen not to be in radical conflict. An angry squire can make all the congregation to be "atheists and tithe-stealers," while an income of five hundred a year may well undermine the plausibility of "any truth, how important soever it may be" that is preached to them.

No, in the end, there is something to be said for Sir Roger's quaint and charming ways, wherein we are "polished and civilized" on Sunday morning, on the seventh day. And, if we are not nodding, like Sir Roger, we can likewise hear the most important truths preached to us in our finery. It is well that we have "our duties explained to us" and finally "to join together in adoration of the Supreme Being."

Chapter 33

"The Pleasure of Learning"

The central thesis of our civilization is found in the following passage from Plato's *Gorgias*: "For no one who is not totally bereft of reason and courage is afraid to die; *doing what's unjust is what he's afraid of.* For of all evils, the ultimate is that of arriving in Hades with one's soul stuffed full of unjust actions" (522e). If this is true, as it is, not a few are "bereft" of reason, but many more of courage. If a good man dies upholding justice, nothing evil has happened to him. The evil rather happens, as we know in the cases of Socrates and Christ, to those who contrive to kill the just man.

Often, it is said that we betray our civilization's basic principle that it is never right to do wrong because of something called "hedonism." Hedonism, of course, as an ideology means that we make our highest good or final end to be pleasure. Aristotle already had noticed this alternative in the first book of his *Ethics*. Pleasure was one of the classic definitions of happiness, or of our final end.

Pleasure is often spoken of as if it is a bad thing, only to be praised in rebuttal by its defenders as the highest of the good things. The fact is that pleasure is a good thing, but not necessarily the highest thing, even when it is good. Pleasure, as the same Aristotle taught, is worth thinking bout.

Not too long ago, a student asked me whether we are made for "happiness." We had just read Aristotle, who held the remarkable opinion that we were. Evidently, the student ran into the view that maintains that we are not really made for happiness, what with the suffering and evil and all.

I suggest that we suspect that we are made for happiness because of our relation to pleasure. How is it that certain particular things actually please us, while others do not? Some thinkers deny that we are made for happiness because that would be, well, selfi The only reason we seek God or anything else, they say, is because we want something for ourselves. The truth is that we do want something. If we already had it, we would not have to worry about seeking it. The idea that benevolence, the doing good to others, means that ultimately we want nothing for ourselves is simply silly. It is not selfish to want for ourselves what is to be wanted.

Someplace I once heard of an experiment – in Nozick's book, I think. It supposed that we were hooked up to new-fangled stimulus machine from which we could receive every pleasure without actually having the experience that is originally designed to produce it. The question is: Would we still want the original experience if we had the pleasure without it? Obviously, we would. A world of pleasure alone is not a world of being in which pleasure is what accompanies, but does not define, what we are and do. Pleasure follows upon an action and "completes" it, not the other way around.

The title of this column is "the pleasure of learning." The title, of course, comes from Plato, as do so many good things. In the ninth book of the *Republic*, we read: "What about the honor-lover? Doesn't he think that the pleasure of making money is vulgar and that *the pleasure of learning* – except as brings him honor – is smoke and nonsense" (581e). But we love learning, knowing, not for the honor we receive from this same knowing, but for itself, its own pleasure.

"A rich man is honored by many people, so is a courageous one, and a wise one," Socrates continued, "but the pleasure of studying the things *that are* cannot be tasted by anyone except a philosopher" (582c). That is to say, we won't even see *the things that are* unless we look for them for their own sakes, unless we discipline the deviations and temptations that keep our attention mostly on ourselves. Yet, there is a pleasure in knowing, just knowing.

Doesn't this sound like few philosophers are found among us, so that very few know reality as such? Plato suspected that most professional "philosophers" and experts were sophists. They were in the knowledge business for money or honor, not for the truth.

In Plato's *Euthydemus*, we read, "After all, we ought to admire every man who says anything sensible, and who labors bravely in its pursuit" (306d). I like that passage. I do admire any man who says anything "sensible" and who labors bravely in its pursuit. Knowing, being sensible, is its own pleasure.

Truth, Plato often said, is to say of *what is* that it is. This knowing of truth results in its own delight. What is not ourselves becomes ourselves. Do we not want this truth also for ourselves? Of course we do. It is on this basis that we rejoice in the philosopher and the sensible man who labor bravely and delightedly in the knowing of *what is*.

Chapter 34

On the Effects of Vice

Virtues and vices are habits, modifications of our activities brought about by our choosing to do things objectively good or bad. Vice is a settled bad habit. We have so guided ourselves in our free actions that we spontaneously do the wrong or bad thing because we want to live this way. Hence, vice implies that, though still possible to do so, we no longer question our acts. We define our happiness in such a way that a wrong end is associated with all our free acts. All other moral acts are affected by our vices.

Once we have acquired a vice by our free decisions, everything we do is seen through its focus. If, say, we make money the primary definition of our happiness, we will use our intelligence or our pleasures or pains to enhance our end. Prudence will mean how we use our minds to select means to possess more wealth. By a criterion of money, we choose our friends or the schools we attend. This vice blinds us so that we no longer see or question the context in which wealth is seen as a good but not the only good. Vice, in short, corrupts our souls by directing all we do to a purpose that itself ought to be examined and ordered.

In Tolkien's *The Two Towers,* we find a striking example of what happens when we select a deviant end that governs all we do. Legolas, Gimli, and Aragorn have been looking for the two abducted hobbits, Merry and Pippin. The three are trying to figure out the nature of their enemy. Suddenly, the wizard Gandalf, whom they thought destroyed, reappears. Gandalf has superior wisdom, but even he does not know everything. Moreover, they all know that dark powers are arrayed against them. However, the evil mind, for all its angelic-like powers, does not anticipate everything, especially kindness and joy. We recall further the old principle that good can know both itself and evil, but evil cannot know good.

The dwarf, the elf, and the man in the group are perplexed. In spite of their need to hurry on in pursuit of those who had captured the hobbits, themselves actually safe for the moment with the Ents, they seek to understand what is happening. They are particularly concerned with the power of Saruman, the shrewd devil-like figure in opposition to them. Gandalf explains the mind of Saruman. This fallen wizard sees everything in terms of his own assumptions about reality, a fatal flaw that provides space for the drama of the insignificant small of this world to have their place. Gandalf speaks of the Ring that has strange powers, especially the power of corruption for those who desire to use its power. However, currently Frodo Baggins, the hobbit, possesses the Ring. He understands that the only safety for the world is to prevent this Ring from falling into the hands of the evil powers, who themselves compete for it.

Here is Gandalf 's analysis of vice, of the effect on an angelic soul when it chooses to make its own power its central mission in its life:

> The Enemy of course has long known that the Ring is abroad, and that it is borne by a hobbit. He knows now the number of our Company.... He does not yet perceive our purpose clearly. He supposes that we were all going to Minas Tirith; for that is what he himself would have done in our place. And according to his wisdom it would have been a heavy stroke against his power. Indeed, he is in great fear, not knowing what mighty one may suddenly appear, wielding the Ring... seeking to cast him down and take his place. That we should wish to cast him down and have *no* one in his place is not a thought that occurs to his mind. That we should wish to destroy the Ring itself has not yet entered into his darkest dream.

The evil power is being consistent with himself. That is, he must assume that everyone else has his same principles, that anyone would do what he would do to obtain the Ring and its power. He cannot imagine a choice not to possess the same power as one's defining purpose. Thus, he cannot see reality or good.

This is the power of vices of any sort. They cause us to see everything in the image of our self-defined end. Hence we miss reality and end up only with ourselves. We cannot imagine a world in which our chosen end is not everyone's chosen end. Thus, the penalty of vice is the living our lives out in terms of the vice, in terms of not seeing what is really good in comparison to our chosen goal.

Chapter 35

"On Responsibility
for Changing Our Souls"

"Repentance and Self-Limitation in the Life of Nations" was a 1974 essay of Alexander Solzhenitsyn. This essay is included in the ISI Books handsome new edition, *The Solzhenitsyn Reader*, 2006. In this essay, the Russian philosopher remarks: "Man's hope, salvation, and punishment lie in this, that we are capable of change, and that we ourselves, not our birth or our environment, are responsible for our souls!" (532). Solzhenitsyn here identifies himself with the Platonic and Christian notion of free will. Rejected is the idea from at least Rousseau that our environment or our civilization establishes what we call good and evil.

"The Blessed Augustine" are the first words of this essay. That is, if we say that 1) our hope, 2) our salvation, and 3) our punishment are rooted in our wills, as the Blessed Augustine taught, we do not intend thereby to deny our need for grace. Our wills do not themselves formulate what is hope, salvation, or punishment. Rather, having insight into what they are as already given from outside of ourselves, we choose to accept them or not. In such choices lies the drama of our existence.

Such dramas take place in all souls regardless of time or place, of polity or economic condition, of whether we are male or female, Jew or Gentile, Greek or Barbarian, learned or dull. This is why great novels can be written of farm life in Nebraska or Kentucky, or of court life in Moscow, or of English families that visit Bath, or of sailors who mutiny at sea.

What is striking in Solzhenitsyn's sentence is the juxtaposing of hope, salvation, and punishment. None of these, evidently, is achieved without the participation of our own souls. Elaborate philosophic and psychological screens work to prevent us from properly locating responsibility in ourselves. Oftentimes, "forces" seem to be at work in the world whose main purpose is to prevent us from understanding ourselves, understanding our destiny.

But what does "hope" have to do with our free will? If we acknowledge no transcendent purpose open to us, we take the first step in locking ourselves solely within our own concepts of good and evil. Thinking there can be no other source, we end up claiming our own omnipotence.

What is the relation of "salvation" to our free will? The latter is the very condition of the former. Salvation, that is, what we would really want if we could have it, has, in human history, many proposals put before us. The only one that really makes sense is the one that includes a free will component in its very description. We are made for a transcendent good that is given to us. We do not constitute it. We are offered it but only on the condition that we trust in what is given to us.

"Punishment" follows from our freedom. The main punishment that we receive both in this life and in eternity is that we permanently live with our choices. Volumes have been written chastising God for "threatening" us with punishment if we do not, say, obey the commandments. Yet, what the Ten Commandments and the two great commandments really do is not punish us, but prevent us from being self-punished.

Obedience to commandments is not a punishment but a freedom to do what we would want to do if we only look at what is at stake in their observance and in their violation. No more terrible punishment can be imagined than the one we give ourselves when we concoct and choose a definition of the world that is not that which caused us to be in the first place.

"We are capable of change." "We ourselves are responsible for our souls."

Imagine the opposite: "We are *not* capable of change. We are *not* responsible for our souls. Change is determined. What happens to us is always someone else's or something else's fault or responsibility. Punishment is always unjust because we are never responsible for what we do."

We do not ourselves cause *what is* to be. We are not the objects of our own hope but we are its subjects. We do not establish what is our destiny, but we do receive it. The ultimate punishment is what we choose to define our own destiny to be apart from what is revealed to us. The glory of the universe is that free beings exist within it. Without these latter, without their being responsible for their own choices, there would be no universe in the first place.

Chapter 36

"To Save His People from Their Sins"

While staying in the rectory of the St. Thomas Aquinas Newman Club at the University of North Dakota, on the shelves of the guest room I noticed the B.A.C. edition of Aquinas's *Summa Theologiae*. I had seen this edition before.

With a few moments to spare, I took down the Third Part of the *Summa*, the volume devoted to Christ. This third part has a brief Prologue explaining its purpose. Unless we pay attention, the very structure of the *Summa* will seem strange to us. How to put it? In the first question that follows this Prologue, Aquinas asks not "whether the Incarnation was necessary" but whether it was "convenient." If it was merely "convenient," but not "necessary," then the Incarnation did not need to happen. If it did not "need" to happen, but did happen, then we must wonder why it happened in terms other than necessity.

What does this "did not need to happen" mean? Evidently, it means that God could have redeemed the human race in a way other than through the Incarnation of one of the Persons of the Trinity, the Word, the Son. The import of Aquinas's question then is clearly, "Why was it done this way, through the Incarnation?" That is, can we, stimulated by the fact of the Incarnation, find a reason for it that makes sense, perhaps the highest sense? Still, it must be a reason that does not make this Incarnation "necessary," as if God were determined to use this way and no other. This restriction leads us to wonder what is higher than "necessity?"

In an essay on the structure of the *Summa*, the great Dominican theologian, M-D Chenu, wrote:

> The vision of God is realized only by and in Christ. Still, to Saint Thomas's way of thinking, our knowledge of God must be examined first in its own inner structure and demands before we can appreciate all the precious and manifold Christ-like ways in which it may manifest itself. The Word, made flesh for our ransoming, is the heart and soul, so to say, of the economy of our Christian

redemption; yet the basic source of the understandableness of this economy (to minds such as ours, at any rate) is precisely its property of being a *via* or means. To see it thus inserted within the ontological framework of grace is not to lessen its inestimable value as a fact of history, unfolding in time (*Thomist Reader*, 1958).

What this explanation implies is that our philosophical and theological understanding of God does not tell us what God, as a free and personal being, will do in an actual world that He created but did not need to create. He will achieve His purposes in His own way in dealing with creatures who are really free, that is, with us.

Thus, to return to Aquinas's Prologue, he begins by citing the passage of the Angel in Matthew (1:24). Christ came to "save His people from their sins." So we begin with a factual historical situation from Genesis. The actual existing race of men whom Christ came to save has a history in which men are mired because of their sins. This is a fact. They need a "way" out of their lot that they cannot achieve or imagine by their own powers, individual or collective. Yet, they still know by natural reasoning even before Christ's Incarnation what is right and wrong but they cannot seem to practice it. What they need is precisely a divine response to their situation, one that respects the freedom of both man and God.

Christ first demonstrates to us that the way of truth is Himself, the point Benedict make in *Jesus of Nazareth*. Through His rising again to immortal life, we are able to perceive the significance of the whole theological enterprise. But we can do this only after having first considered what we can know with our human reason about the ultimate end of human life and of the virtues and vices. This consideration was the subject of the earlier two books of the *Summa*. With this background, we can consider and seek to understand as much as we can of this very Savior and His benefices to the human race.

We thus first consider what the Savior is, then the sacraments by which salvation it attained, and finally the end of immortal life to which, through this very resurrection, we arrive. Since the purpose of the Savior coming is "to save the people from their sins," the structure of the Incarnation, as it were, takes places through the consequences of these sins. The way that God in His Trinitarian reasoning decides to save us is not through power or necessity, but through our freedom and the divine freedom.

Aquinas's question was whether it was "convenient" that we were redeemed in a peculiar way, through the Incarnation, life and death of the God-man. It need not have happened this way. What was the *via*, the way, in which it did happen? We were shown the consequences of our sins by this God-man who is Christ suffering for us. We remain free to accept or reject this way.

But it is a way that is in conformity with the highest in us and in God. It is a way that does not "force" us to be free, but one that invites us to be free. The initiative of God in the Incarnation and Redemption stems from something beyond justice and necessity. It is the intervention of a love for us that does not seek to save us by overpowering us. Rather on seeing the consequences of our sins in Christ, it invites us to understand and choose. It is indeed a most "convenient" way.

Chapter 37

On the Inn at the End of the World

No passage in Chesterton has, over the years, haunted me more than the passage that ends *Dickens*. He writes these memorable lines: "The inn does not point to the road; the road points to the inn. And all roads point at last to an ultimate inn, where we shall meet Dickens and all his characters: and when we drink again it shall be from the great flagons in the tavern at the end of the world." No abstraction permitted here.

One morning, just before Christmas, when I had finished grading most of my examinations, I had some time. So I looked through a pile of Chesterton books. For no reason I pulled out the *Selected Essays of G. K. Chesterton*. This book of essays was selected by Dorothy Collins, first published October 20, 1949, by Methuen in the Strand in London.

Looking at the Table of Contents, I noticed the third essay. It was entitled, "The End of the World," originally found in *Tremendous Trifles*, in 1909. I am sure I have seen this essay before. I have noted that this theme of the inn at the end of the world not infrequently comes up in varying ways in Chesterton. I read it with particular delight.

The essay recounts a stay of Chesterton in the French city of BesanHon in eastern France, south of Dijon. This famous town goes back to the time of Caesar. Chesterton remarked that the local guidebooks tell us that Victor Hugo was born there and that the city was of military consequence. But they seem to miss the mystery of the place, a city built almost as an island surrounded by a river.

Chesterton is outside a café. Along comes a huge Frenchman driving a "fly," a small carriage. They converse. Chesterton begins to compare this Frenchman with Falstaff. This reflection leads to the difference between the English and French character. The man offers to take Chesterton for a ride up into the high rocky countryside. As they leave the city gate, Chesterton hears three sounds that seem to him to epitomize France. The first is a brass band playing tunes from Parisian comic operas in the Casino gardens, playing with "passionate levity," as he puts it. He also hears the bugles of the army in the hills, and finally, midst it all, the Angelus.

On leaving in the Frenchman's fly-cart, Chesterton had the feeling of having "left France behind… or perhaps the civilized world." He does not quite understand where the big Frenchman is taking him. He is a bit dizzy from the circular climb. Finally, Chesterton asks him, "Where are you taking me?" The man did not turn around. "To the end of the world," he replies.

Chesterton is silent. They continue the climb in the evening light. They come to a tiny village. Suddenly, Chesterton recognizes its name on the walls of the local inn, *Le Bout du Monde* – "the end of the world." The two men sit down outside the inn. They do not speak a word, "as if all ceremonies were natural and understood in that ultimate place." Bread and wine are ordered. Across is a small church. On its steeple was a cross, on top of which is a rooster. Chesterton says, rather prophetically, "This seemed to me a very good end of the world; if the story of the world ended here it ended well."

But Chesterton wondered to himself if the world did end here, whether he himself would be content in this place. Certainly, he acknowledged, that here are found "the best things of Christendom." What are these? A "church and children's games and decent soil and a tavern for men to talk with men." He had seen some children playing ball on the way in. And all philosophy exists in conversation, preferably in taverns and inns. Even Socrates seemed to imply something like this conversation in his reference to immortality at the end of his *Apology*.

Still, Chesterton was not satisfied. This was a "French" end of the world. He wanted to be driven to an English "end of the world." An Englishman belongs at the English end of the world. The French driver is puzzled. "'The other end of the world,' he asked, 'Where is that?'" Chesterton professed his love for the French vines and free peasantry, but he preferred the English end of the world. Where was that? It was at "Walham Green"; you could pass it in a London omnibus. He liked the Frenchman well enough. "I love you like a brother, but I want an English cabman, who will be funny and ask me what his fare 'is.'" French bugles stir him but he wants to see a London policeman.

The two return to BesanHon, as the Frenchman cannot be expected to take him to England in such a conveyance. "You will understand," Chesterton explains to him, "if ever you are an exile, even for pleasure."

The last sentence of this remarkable essay is as follows: "Only as the stars came out among those immortal hills I wept for Walham Green."

Evidently, several decades ago, the name, Walham Green, was unconscionably changed to "Fulham Broadway" by those who had no clue of where they lived. I do not know, or want to know, why people at the end of the English world know not where they are. Thus the only place the English "end of the world" still exists is in an essay about an inn named *Le Bout du Monde* in a hamlet high above the river Doubs surrounding BesanHon.

What was once found there – the church, the children playing, the vines, the tavern in which men could talk to men – were, indeed, "the best things of Christendom." All roads point to that ultimate inn where, as Chesterton also put it in *Dickens*, "comradeship and serious joy are not interludes in our travel; but that rather our travels are interludes in comradeship and joy, which through God shall endure for ever."

This passage must explain, I think, why Chesterton had said to the Frenchman in his perfect inn, in *Le Bout du Monde*, "you will understand if ever you are an exile, even for pleasure." We are all, as Scripture tells us often, but "sojourners and exiles" seeking to understand what is there at the end of the world, of our world, be we Frenchmen above BesanHon, Englishmen at Walham Green, or ourselves in whatever particular, very particular place in which we find ourselves. The end of the world, the best things of Christendom, finally exist no place else but here.

Chapter 38

On Lying to One's Soul

Wearing his baseball cap and uniform, Charlie Brown comes into his living room, where his sister Sally sits watching TV on her bean-bag seat. Dejectedly, Charlie says to her, "It's the last game of the season, and we lost." Sally just walks away, saying to a puzzled Charlie, "So what does that mean?" With his hat to the side of his head and Sally nowhere in sight, he explains aloud philosophically, "Well in the long run and as far as the rest of the world goes, it doesn't mean a thing...." In the last scene, however, Charlie's head is buried despondently in the bean bag. He laments, "But I can't stand it" (Schulz, *If Beagles Could Fly*, 1990).

No doubt, we cannot but see something noble in Charlie Brown's refusal to admit that the game and the season are not important, even though he knows Sally does not care and the game doesn't mean a thing "to the rest of the world."

No one should be surprised if I tell him that this end-of-the-season scene reminds me of Plato. Everything reminds me of something in Plato. The *Peanuts* incident recalls a passage near end of the second book of *The Republic*. I read this passage aloud to a class, it struck me so much. It recalls Charlie's realization that some things are important even if no one else thinks so. There is something poignant about suffering for a real loss that no one else figures to mean anything. But with Charlie's "can't stand it," we see that he recognizes a real loss, even if it is only not winning the last game of the season.

The conversation between Socrates and Adeimantus had been about whether the gods would lie. But when Socrates asks him whether the gods would "lie," Adeimantus replies lamely that he "does not know." Next, Socrates asks him, "don't you know that all gods and men hate a true lie?" Adeimantus still does not get what Socrates is driving at. Surely, Socrates explains, "no one wants to lie about the most serious things" in the deepest part of his own soul. Indeed, in this inner place is where we fear a lie most of all.

Lying to ourselves about *the things that are*, about the most important things, is surely a most provocative concern. We suddenly realize is that we can lie to ourselves about the nature of our being, of our world. We can choose *not* to know *what is* in order that we do not have to change our ways.

Socrates continues, "to lie and to have lied to the soul about *the things that are...* and to have a lie there is what everyone would least accept, and that everyone hates a lie in that place (his own soul) most of all."

If it were true that no one lied to himself about reality, the world would be a pretty good place. Socrates, of course, is speaking of the city he is building in speech, of those who are as they ought to be. He knows of the discrepancy between the things that are actually done and the things that ought or ought not to be done. Like Charlie's lost game, it seems that nobody in the world cares about the things of one's soul.

Yet, Socrates' words are, "no one would want a lie in his soul" about the most important things.

The notion of lying to ourselves is deliberately paradoxical. Lying normally refers to what we tell others that is not in conformity with what we hold or know. The possibility of lying to ourselves is more subtle. It means that we can control our picture of the world so that it does not conform to reality.

Socrates suggests that we can lie to ourselves in the most important things, not just in little or indifferent things. Lying to ourselves about the most important things defines what we are before these same important things. Does this mean that the drama of our existence is not exterior to ourselves after all? Indeed, it does. Moreover, we control the drama.

Charlie Brown, as manager of the losing team, does not lie to himself. He knows his team loses. He does not pretend that they win when they lost. Charlie's soul is not divided within himself. This is the drama of his "I can't stand it."

But Plato's admonition remains. No one wants a lie in his soul about *the things that are*. Yet, the implication remains. It is possible to reject in our souls the order of things. We can refuse to see because we do not want to know the truth in our souls if this truth requires of us what we refuse to give. Ultimately, this lie in our souls is what we "cannot stand."

Chapter 39

Existence: "Cherish it!"

In 1911, Chesterton spoke to a club in Cambridge calling themselves "The Heretics," whether after the title of Chesterton's 1905 book of the same title, I am not sure. Chesterton actually came mildly to chastise these students for this title, which at first seems so haughtily rebellious. In a letter from Beaconsfield in 1912, he told them that "here were many sorts of questions I should like to have asked the Heretics, if they had not asked so many questions of me. But, first and last, I should like to ask them why they are so weak-minded (if you will forgive the phrase) as to admit that they *are* Heretics. You never really think your own opinion right until you can call it Orthodox." In the midst of 21st century relativism that is a refreshing phrase, "to think our own opinions right."

Chesterton's talk was given in the Cambridge Guild Hall in response to a lecture the previous year by George Bernard Shaw on "The Future of Religion." These remarks of Chesterton were summarized in the *Cambridge Magazine* on January 12, 1912, and reprinted in *The Chesterton Review* for August of 1986. The article consists in a summary of Chesterton's talk and a record of a question and answer session with students and faculty. Chesterton is always at his most amusing best in these situations.

Recalling 18th century religion, Chesterton remarks that "in France, Louis XVI, who happened to be a sincere Catholic, almost pleaded with his Ministers and advisers that he might be excused from appointing an atheist to the archbishopric of Paris" (288). What sort of an atheist might we have who would accept such an appointment! And this brings Chesterton to Dr. Samuel Johnson, perplexed in the same age for almost the opposite reason. "In England in the eighteenth century Dr. Johnson was largely considered a portent, an extraordinary being, because he went to Church and had brains." As I think of this remark, I realize that is the best definition of Catholicism I can think of – someone who goes to Mass and has brains.

As to the debate itself, Chesterton addressed Shaw's idea of "heretics." Evidently, Shaw said that "heretics were people who found a machine, such as a motor-car, and by tinkering at it turned it into something else." They would be heretics, I take it, because the prevailing idea is that we cannot change a motor-car into anything but a motor-car. Chesterton, to laughter, said of this position of Shaw that "he knew it sounded funny, but it was down in the lecture." This is what the man said. What did it mean? This puzzled Chesterton who did not mind "if anybody could find a sewing machine lying about and turn it into an old high bicycle... but he strongly objected to their finding a bicycle and turning it into a sewing machine, and then trying to ride the sewing machine" (290). In logic, the "heretical" position had the drawback of being reduced to silliness on its own premises. However romantic heresy might be, orthodoxy, as he told the students, has the advantage of the firm opinion that we cannot ride a sewing machine.

Shaw seems to have had the idea that God is somehow trying to come into existence but hasn't quite yet made it. God, Chesterton thought on the contrary, must already be. "There must be first a fixed ideal." Shaw's ideal is precisely "unfixed." "What was the good of a God which was gradually trying to exist?" Not merely what was the "good" of such a god, but what was the sense of it? "There was no such thing as trying to exist. They had to exist before they tried" (291). Being is before becoming. A god who is "not yet" cannot at the end of a process turn around, look at himself, and say that "this is what I intended to become" unless he already intended to become what which he intended. That would make him a "fixed point," however.

When it came to summing up the essentials of the "old Christian theory," Chesterton said, again to applause, that there were two main points: "The first idea was that if God set humanity free He could not keep them bound; the second was that the idea of setting the people free as so inspiring a conception that it would excuse man, or God, or any other being, in facing all the risks and troubles of the world. That was the Christian religion." (294). If God made free beings, He could not in the same act turn around and bind them so that their freedom was not a part of their very relation to God. Once we recognize that there are free beings in the universe, including God's freedom in making rather than not making it, what follows is the drama, the "risks and troubles of the world." It is not a defect in God that there are free beings, nor that these free beings, using their own creative powers, can also reject God. This is how Chesterton put the same point later in the question period:

> The doctrine of Liberty was that the Creator made something which could also create in its turn. That was ordinary logic. If they said that God could at the same time keep men bound and prevent their going wrong they were mystic, they were confusing terms, and were not using Reason. If they admitted the Liberty was desirable and that Reason constrained things, then they had the Christian doctrine of Free Will (297).

God could create beings who could act freely. Their guidance was also a self-guidance according to reason.

In the question and answer period, Chesterton is asked about Pascal and the Jesuits. "Pascal denied that Reason could lead one to God and that Liberty was possible. It was because the Catholic Church was on the side of Reason and Liberty that it suppressed Pascal and the Janssenists." Chesterton then wanted to know, "did anyone in the room know what Pascal was arguing with the Jesuits about?" Here is Chesterton's explication of the argument. "The Jesuits said that God really wanted every man to be good, to escape hell, and to save his soul. Pascal said that God deliberately damned some people, that he deliberately meant that some people should not have the grace to enable them to overcome their temptations" (295). Chesterton then looks at the audience to ask, wryly, "On which side were his hearers?"

A final encounter, a "passage-at-arms," also caused considerable amusement and insight. This is the old epistemological question revisited. A questioner said that "Mr. Chesterton could not say he knew a thing unless he had scientific proof of it." The questioner thus maintained that he would never say "I know," but only that "I have an intuition." Chesterton then asked him, "You know you exist?" The man denied it, protesting that he could not use the phrase "I know." He preferred to say "I have an intuition that I exist."

Chesterton replied that it was too bad, but that he, Chesterton, could himself say, "I know, I am absolutely certain, that I exist." Moreover, Chesterton said that the gentleman knew "that he existed." It is foolish to say that we could not be certain of anything about which we do not have scientific proof. The questioner replies that it is merely a question of "definition." The gentleman says that he uses the word "know" in a different sense. He tries to save himself by affirming: "I say it is perfectly true that I have an intuition that I exist." To this Chesterton merely quips, "Cherish it." There follows "laughter and applause." Existence is safe.

And this "cherishing" brings us back to the very point of a "fixed point." It is the same thing to say that "I know I exist" and to say, with some convolutedness, "it is perfectly true that I have an intuition that I exist." God exists. He does not try to exist. Nothing is clearer than that cherished affirmation that "I exist."

"The Jesuits said that God really wanted every man to be good, to escape hell, and to save his soul." "You never really think your own opinion right until you call it orthodox." Atheists should be excused from the archbishopric of Paris. A man can "go to Church and have brains." A man who turns a bicycle into a sewing machine may be a "heretic," but the man who understands that he cannot ride a sewing machine remains "orthodox," because he still sees things as they are.

Chapter 40

"Ultimate Knowledge upon the Ultimate Realities"

In 1927, Macmillan published a book by the Dominican philosopher, Vincent McNabb, entitled *The Catholic Church and Philosophy*. McNabb was a friend of Hilaire Belloc, whom he asked to write a brief "Preface" to the book. Belloc's "Preface" contains many points that are now found in John Paul II's *Fides et Ratio*, a document designed to address the condition both of philosophy in the present culture and of the importance of philosophy to Catholicism.

Belloc began his short essay by remarking that the one branch of knowledge that one would think "specifically pointed" to an area of interest to Catholicism, namely, philosophy, was most often seen as in "conflict" with it or "neglected" by it. However, at least one of the "peculiar functions" of the Catholic Church was to "preserve the philosophic conquests of pagan antiquity and to expand them over an even greater range of discovery than the greatest of the ancients had commanded." This is a remarkable sentence.

If the philosophic "conquests" of the ancients were to be preserved, it must imply that at least some of them were true, were worth preserving. But the other side of this preservation was to "discover" new understandings of reality using these same principles. This implied, however, that there was something in Catholicism that could add to, expand, the understanding of these valid principles.

Religious conflict, Belloc thought, caused this relationship of philosophy to Catholicism to be obscured. Yet, everyone would grant that, say, in art or architecture, the religious experience of these traditions did add to their perfection. How account for this opinion that Catholicism did not also add to philosophy?

The problem has to do with the idea of "discovery," Belloc thought. In the modern world, the term "philosophy" has acquired a meaning quite different from its usage by the ancients or Christians. "Philosophy,"

Belloc succinctly comments, "signifies primarily the love of knowledge – *ultimate knowledge upon the ultimate realities*; and, by extension, it especially signifies *the solving of questions which the mind puts to itself relative to the most important subjects with which the mind can deal.*"

Man is a question-asking animal. Most people would have no problem with this affirmation. But it is peculiar to modernity, largely because of epistemological problems, to deny that any question, especially questions about the "ultimate realities," can have any coherent answers. What is clear for someone reading St. Thomas, for example, is that not only does he ask thousands of questions, he proposes thousands of answers, with reasons for his answers. With revelation, we are not as content, or at least not content in the same way, with Socrates' "knowing that we do not know." But there was no doubt that the ancients did ask penetrating questions about the highest things.

The term "discovery" means the processes or argument by which we find an answer to a question as asked. "A process of reasoning which establishes the existence of a personal God is a *discovery*." Belloc thinks that discovering a new philosophic truth is as important as discovering the planet Pluto or a physical law.

At first sight, many ultimate questions seem to be insolvable. This mood of frustration over the multiple contradictory answers given in philosophy gave rise to sophistry, as the Greeks called it. Sophistry meant giving answers just to be giving answers. It meant spinning out answers that seemed consistent or logical but which were really wrong or ungrounded. Sophistry, Belloc explains, "is the art of making up systems which do not really solve problems and which are hardly intended to do so by their authors, which are, in a word, not discoveries, but merely guesses at the best, or at the worst a mass of verbiage." A "mass of verbiage" would be a system with no basis in reality.

The sophist is the man who does not care about the truth or falsity of his position. He claims to be able to teach any system, whatever the questioner demands, usually for a fee. That is, he himself, the sophist, is not bound by any objective order of reality that would correspond or claim to correspond to his words. Indeed, he does not think there is such a thing as truth. This methodic doubt leaves him free to spin out any confi h e chooses, in secret or in public. The most dangerous sophists are those who seek to impose what is in effect their imaginations onto reality as if it were real. The sophist can teach the politician, hence the danger multiplied.

Belloc thought that this "sort of stuff," as he called it, has flourished since the end of the 18th century, especially in Germany. It is what most people today call "philosophy," a "theory" not a reality. The sophist, for instance, is someone who maintains that "there are no ultimate contradictions; any two apparently contradictory things may be resolved into a higher unity." Belloc calls such a position a "fog"! It sounds very much like Hegel, a German, to be sure.

The "glory of the Catholic Church," Belloc concludes, is "to have insisted throughout her existence upon the treatment of the gravest questions in a philosophical manner." And also, since the 12th century, to have developed a "scheme of exploration" whereby some criterion of asking and answering such questions is in place. Since all of this questioning and answering has been going on for centuries, this genuine philosophic discovery must be seen for what it is.

At the time of the neo-Thomist period in which he wrote, Belloc could see some increasing interest in true philosophy. We are not looking for "the incomprehensible, the vague, nor the evading of questions in a mist of words, but research, discovery, and consequent rational and exact explanation."

What is to be noted in this brief philosophical preface of Belloc is his awareness of "discovery" and its criterion. He understood that valid questions were asked by the ancient philosophers, by Plato, Aristotle, and the Stoics. When these very questions were taken up in the light of revelation, they did not become less urgent or less necessary. Indeed, unless the questions were asked, unless the answers the ancient thinkers gave to them were known, no one would realize that the answers of revelation were in fact addressed to proper questions that had already arisen.

Modern philosophy is called sophistry to the extent that it systematically denies that our minds can reach reality and reason on this same reality, on *what is*. The charge of sophistry is accurate to the extent that modern philosophical systems do not base themselves on being but upon what the mind concocts for itself without any effort to ground its pronouncements in the valid questions and answers that have been proposed though experiment, reason, and argument.

Philosophy does concern itself with "ultimate knowledge upon the ultimate realities." The Catholic Church is indeed concerned with the philosophy that knows and seeks *what is*. It has insisted "upon the treatment of the gravest questions in a philosophical manner." When this treatment is not present, the education or the consideration is simply not Catholic, because it is not philosophical.

Chapter 41

"On Being Pleased"

Frequently, we read a sentence that we have read before and realize that we have never really "noticed" what it means. We can pronounce "words" but not "understand" them. The verb "to notice" implies that we come across something that we did not ourselves first put there, something that stands out to be seen even before it is seen.

The word "notice" comes from the Latin and Greek words for knowledge – *notitia, gnosis*. That we "know" something implies that what is known exists in two ways, first in its own way of being outside of nothingness and, secondly, also in our inner being. We are not naturally Kantians who suspect everything begins inside of us. We are naturally Aristotelians who know that it doesn't. To "know" means "being" what it is we know, without what we know becoming other than it is. If I know that tree before me exists, the tree itself does not change because I know it. But I do. I *am* suddenly more than I *am*.

What started me off about knowledge was a passage in Aristotle, one I have often read, even marked. It reads: "Being pleased is a condition of the soul" (1099a8). Here, Aristotle talks not about knowledge but about pleasure, a favorite topic of his. Aristotle even says that knowing itself carries with it its own unique pleasure that we neglect at our peril.

Our souls are made "to be pleased." How often have you ever heard someone repeat that astonishing piece of information? We may also be able to please others. But the greater mystery is our own capacity *to be pleased*, almost as if, for our own good, something other than ourselves must already exist. In a sentence translated into but eight English words, we are given the profoundest insight into our very being. *We are beings who can be pleased.*

In 1780, to approach this topic from a different angle, James Boswell was unable to visit Samuel Johnson in London. Instead of his usual account of their conversation in various clubs, pubs, and dinner parties, he obtained the report of their friend Bennet Langton for that year. Reading through Langton's remarks, I came across the following sentence that I do not recall ever having seen before, though it is of profound significance. I am sure that I had previously read it: "*The applause of a single human being is of great consequence*" (II, 355). I almost gasped when I read that sentence. It is Plato. Almost everything is in Plato, and what is not, he already makes us in some sense long for, a longing that no one better understood than Augustine.

If "being pleased is a condition of our soul," being capable of applauding something not ourselves is likewise its manifestation. Applauding ourselves, however, is something rather approaching the diabolical. Moreover, like "being pleased," we do not "applaud" until something happens. Properly speaking, we do not applaud until something over which we have no control is completed, until, that is, we recognize it for what it is, its wonder.

What can it mean to say that the "applause" of a *single* person is of great "consequence." Can a single person be so important? What is good exists so that even one person might recognize it. What is this "applause?" We have all been to concerts. "Applause" is what we do after hearing a lovely symphony at the Kennedy Center. The one essential thing that we must remember is that "applause" cannot be programmed or commanded.

Unless "applause" can be withheld, it is worth little. And "envy" means the refusal to applaud what is worthy to be applauded. Applause must arise "spontaneously," yet appreciatively, almost as if its cause is wholly unanticipated. Applause need not follow performance as if the applause were itself part of the performance. Applause exists in the realm of freedom, not determinism.

Take another look at these two remarkable sentences, the one from Aristotle – "*being pleased is a condition of the soul*" – and the one from Johnson – "*the applause of a single human being is of great consequence.*" "Are these two sentences related?" I wonder. To have a soul capable of "being pleased" means first that our souls are not divine, not their own cause. On the other hand, if the applause of a single human being has consequence, it must mean that the world is full of things worthy of our appreciation, worthy of our *notice*.

The "applause" of a single human being can make any of our lives worth living, make us realize that we are not alone, that something in us is worthy of being noticed and loved. Revelation means being given what is most worthy of our applause.

Chapter 42

On the Temptation to Organize the World

Ogden Nash has a poem that begins, "A man could be granted to live a dozen lives / And he still wouldn't be understood by daughters and wives...." We probably wouldn't want a world in which it were otherwise, a world in which absolutely everything could be understood by husbands and wives. I do not intend to defend mystery here or the finiteness of our intellects, designed to know *all that is*. Rather I want to reflect on what it would mean to claim that we know everything, especially that we create the distinction between good and evil.

On the John Paul II's visit to Poland, June 6, 1999, he took a helicopter to a sea port called Elblag, a city of about 130,000 people. Improbably, in Elblag they had an "Aviation Club," where the Pope participated in devotions at which he recited "the Act of Consecration of the Human Race to the Sacred Heart of Jesus." Makes you wonder that if the Holy Father can consecrate the human race at the Aviation Club in Elblag, it could be done in any parish in the States?

John Paul II explained that "Everything that God wanted to tell us about himself and about his love he placed in the Heart of Jesus, and by means of that Heart he has told us everything." This sentence does not refer to our own views of the world, our own opinions of the important things. What is important is what "God wanted to tell us about himself." The first thing that those who love God must do, recalling John 14:15, is to keep the Commandments. The Ten Commandments are the "foundation of morality." And just to remind us, he proceeded to recite all Ten Commandments, a good practice.

Christ confirmed these Commandments at the Sermon on the Mount. The "whole order of truth" is "inscribed on the human heart." The Pope cited the passages that Christ used to reaffirm the commandments – "I have come not to abolish them (the Law and the Prophets) but to fulfill them" (Matthew, 5:17); "He who has my commandments and keeps them, he it is who loves me; and he who loves me will be loved by my Father" (John, 14:21). The Pope finally cited the passage he loves from Matthew, 19:16, the passage that he reflected on in *Veritatis Splendor*, where the young man asks, "Teacher, what good deed must I do to have eternal life?" Jesus answers, "If you would enter life, keep the Commandments."

At this point, John Paul II paused in his homily to remind us that "This response by Jesus is particularly important in our modern reality, in which many people live as though there were no God." This is not something neutral, or abstract, but something contemporary, quite widespread, perhaps world-wide. It is not just a question of men not being understood by their wives and daughters, but of God being positively rejected.

In what sounds to be a modern "Aviation Club" during what seemed like early modern devotions, the Polish pope added these profound words: "The temptation to organize the world and one's own life without God or even in opposition to God, without his Commandments and without the Gospel, is a very real temptation and threatens us too. When human life and the world are built without God, they will eventually turn against man himself " (*L'Osservatore Romano*, English, 16 June 1999).

So a temptation to attempt to organize ourselves and the world on principles that ignore or reject the Commandments does exist among us. We are in fact undergoing this temptation more and more in our civil laws and personal practices. Once we posit our own will as the source of law and action, as we are free to do, we proceed to live as we choose. No Pope who knows his theology, as John Paul II certainly did, can be surprised that this possibility exists. But notice what he says about this possibility. Who can it hurt? God? It does indeed hurt God through hurting those He loves.

The crux of the issue is that when we build our lives and that of our society without God, without the Commandments, such lives will "turn against man." That is, they will turn against those who observe the Commandments. It is probably no accident that this turning seems almost complete in our public order and that, correspondingly, the Pope more and more talked about martyrdom. Even if we are granted a dozen lives, even if Lazarus returns from the grave, it will not be otherwise if we do not observe the Commandments, because we choose to deny, by our choices and actions, the validity of the law of God in our hearts.

Chapter 43

The Opposite of Funny

The year 2005 was the hundredth anniversary of the publication of Chesterton's *Heretics*. I want to say something about the sixteenth chapter of *Heretics*, which is entitled, "On Mr. McCabe and a Divine Frivolity." In the October 1993 edition of the old *Midwest Chesterton News*, I wrote a column entitled precisely "The Divine Frivolity." I do not have a copy of that column handy, but this chapter is probably its inspiration. However, it is such a good chapter that I think I will write about it again.

Mr. McCabe seems to have been an ex-priest turned writer, a not uncommon phenomenon of the species. Evidently, he had chided Chesterton for being too frivolous and paradoxical about pious things. McCabe did not see any humor in divine things. He did not see much humor in human things either, or at least he did not see how humor could be of serious import. Chesterton, for his part, thought that McCabe did not know that the most solemn things are often the funniest, or occasions for great humor. "Men make jokes about old scientific professors, even more than they make them about bishops – not because science is lighter than religion, but because science is always by its nature more solemn and austere than religion" (*CW*, I, 157).

What Chesterton was most concerned with was the notion that solemnity is a sign of truth, while humor is a sign of falsity. Chesterton held that quite the opposite was really true. Truth lies in lightsomeness and light-heartedness. We can laugh when we know the world was made for joy.

"Mr. McCabe thinks that I am not serious but only funny, because Mr. McCabe thinks that funny is the opposite of serious. Funny is the *opposite of not funny*, and of nothing else" (159). What a wonderful sentence that is! *Funny is the opposite of not funny.* Whether a thing is true or not has nothing to do with whether it is funny or not. The greatest of truths can be found in our humor.

To further confirm this point, Chesterton adds, "Whether a man chooses to tell the truth in long sentences or in short jokes is a problem analogous to whether he chooses to tell the truth in French or German" (160). The question is not the literary form or language one uses, but whether he tells the truth in whatever language he chooses to use. One can, I suppose, lie in a joke also, though Chesterton suspects it is more difficult. "The two qualities of fun and seriousness have nothing whatever to do with each other, they are no more comparable than black and triangular." To think clearly is to make the proper distinctions. This failure is why McCabe was classified as a "heretic." He could not see what his mind was designed to see.

Chesterton next takes McCabe's former ecclesiastical status to say some things about the clergy. Clerics, Chesterton observed, often seem to operate under a "primary fallacy." What is this fallacy? "Numbers of clergy" have reproached him "for making jokes about religion." And to prove that he was frivolous, they cited the commandment not to take the Lord's name "in vain." But to make a joke of something is not taking it "in vain." Quite the contrary. "To use a thing in vain means to use it without use. But a joke may be exceedingly useful; it may contain the whole earthly sense, not to mention the whole heavenly sense, of a situation."

Chesterton pointed out that the ones who really take the Lord's name in vain are "the clergymen themselves" (161). How so? "The thing which is fundamentally and really frivolous is a careless solemnity." You find this frivolity more in the pulpit or the House of Commons than anywhere else. "It is solemnity that is stopping the way in every department of modern life." Paradox and jesting are not the problems.

"In the modern world solemnity is the direct enemy of sincerity. In the modern world, sincerity is almost always on one side and solemnity always on the other. What a prophet or a teacher gives us, Chesterton adds, may or may not be eloquent or witty. From these sources, "we may not expect the true, we may not even expect the wise, but we do expect the unexpected." (162)

Behind Chesterton's "heretic" we always find a philosophical position. McCabe evidently thought that Chesterton's "frivolity" denigrated religion, something that would thereby increase public "sensuality" (163). Chesterton called this view an "error." He predicted rather a decrease in sensuality because the philosophy on which McCabe based his view lacked vitality. "I do not think that under modern Western materialism we should have anarchy. I doubt whether we should have enough individual valour and spirit even to have liberty." The question Chesterton raises is the logic of materialism. What in fact does it allow us to do?

"Our objection to skepticism is that it removes the motive power," Chesterton explains. "Materialism is not a thing which destroys mere restraint. Materialism itself is the great restraint. The McCabe school advocates a political liberty, but it denies spiritual liberty. That is, it abolishes the laws which could be broken, and substitutes laws that cannot. And that is the real slavery." It would be difficult to be more succinct. We are free only if we have laws we can break. By embracing determinism, restraint is abolished. Restraint implies voluntary self-rule. If things *must* happen, even in human affairs, we cannot talk as if we can choose not to do them. No real spiritual freedom exists if we must do what we do. Moral laws can be broken; physical ones cannot.

Chesterton next relates this determinism to the political order. "The truth is that the scientific civilization in which Mr. McCabe believes has one rather particular defect; it is perpetually tending to destroy that democracy or power of the ordinary man in which Mr. McCabe also believes. Science means specialism, and specialism means oligarchy." This habit of mind of leaving things to specialists in science leads to the notion that you can do the same thing in politics. "Once men sang together round a table in chorus; now one man sings alone, for the absurd reason that he can sing better. If scientific civilization goes on (which is improbable) only one man will laugh, because he can laugh better than the rest" (164). Of course, this is Chesterton's doctrine that, in some things, like blowing our noses, voting, singing, and dancing, we want everyone to participate or do it themselves, even if he does it badly.

"I should regard any civilization which was without a universal habit of uproarious dancing as being, from the full human point of view, a defective civilization," Chesterton concluded. "And I should regard any mind which had not got the habit in one form or another of uproarious thinking as being, from the full human point of view, a defective mind.... Unless a man is in part a humourist, he is only in part a man" (166). A solemnity that cannot, in principle, also break into laughter and joy, either because of determinism or habit, is, ultimately, not worth having.

Actually, this chapter on the "divine frivolity" in *Heretics* is a kind of apologia of Chesterton's own style and philosophy. "If Mr. McCabe asks me why I import frivolity into a discussion of the nature of man, I answer, because frivolity is a part of the nature of man. If he asks me why I introduce what he calls paradoxes into a philosophical problem, I answer, because all philosophical problems tend to become paradoxical." A paradox is a statement that seems to go against common sense but which may well be true. It seems paradoxical to say that there is frivolity and joy, and not just solemnity, in the divinity. But it just might be true, and if it is, as Chesterton always implies, our whole attitude to the world is not a matter of determinism, but a matter of a freedom in which our choices make a difference because they constitute part of the nature of man.

Chapter 44

The Verses of Empedocles

Aristotle tells us that, to knowledge, there is its own pleasure. Though we have perhaps experienced this pleasure, we seldom reflect on its significance. Indeed, Aristotle tells us that not to experience the pleasure that comes from knowing is itself rather a dangerous thing. Since the pleasure of a thing is indicative of the worthiness of a thing, to miss the delight of intellect is usually to miss the delight of knowing. The one who lacks this latter, Aristotle thought, will usually go off into rather disordered pleasures, or pleasures separated from the proper activities in which they should exist.

Chesterton says someplace that we should memorize great poetry before we know what it means so that, once we have enough experience of life to understand it, we will already have the exalted words that poets have used to express it. In an age without books or computers, the only way to retain something written by someone else was for ourselves to memorize it. We can memorize words that we do not know, especially if they sound good, but still not know that these same words contain profound things that we would love to know.

When I read and reread Aristotle, I always find something that I had not reflected enough about. I know that a given passage in question was worth thinking about, for I had underlined it in my previous readings. This Spring, for example, on rereading Aristotle, I came across the following passage from Book VII of the *Ethics*, on the intellectual virtues, on the truth of things: "Saying the words that come from knowledge is no sign of having it. For people affected to these ways (i.e., having the words) even recite demonstrations and *verses of Empedocles*. Further, those who have just learnt something do not yet know it, though they string the words together, for it must grow into them, and this needs time" (1147a18–23).

Thus, I can say or recite the words of a poem, or a proof in geometry, or a passage in Aquinas without knowing what it means. The point is not that it is a bad thing to know words without understanding. It may be a very good thing, as Chesterton implied in memorizing a poem before we fully grasp its meaning. It is wonderful to have the "verses of Empedocles" or the lines of Sophocles or Shakespeare in our memory. That is its own art.

But Aristotle goes on to his main point, that when we just learn something, the words or the demonstration, "we do not yet *know* it." We do "string the words together." Still we must "grow into them." This takes time and experience. Many things exist outside of us that we do not see till, inside, we are ready to see them. The inner formation of our souls is itself a requirement for us before we see the depths of the reality that we confront every day. And every day we encounter realities that are worth knowing, only we do not have the time or the wit to see what is there, to see *what is*.

The penalty for not caring for our souls is the-not-knowing-reality, especially the reality of those we would know and love.

I clipped out a "Classic Peanuts" the other day. In one long strip, Charlie Brown, Linus, and Lucy are on the floor, each with a coloring book, each with boxes of crayons, many of which are scattered on the floor. With a concerned look, Charlie reads out loud from a newspaper. "It says here that the average child wears down 730 crayons before he or she is ten years old." Snoopy sits next to Charlie but looks at Linus, who is lying on his stomach, intently coloring. Charlie continues, with a fine piece of pop sociology, "And that coloring promotes understanding and brings children closer together."

At this point, testing the theory, Linus asks, "What color should I make the sky?" Meantime, Lucy has her back to both of them. Without looking up from her own coloring, she replies, *"Blue, you blockhead!"* Such is the worth of the thesis that coloring with crayons promotes "understanding" and "brings children together."

What's this got to do with memorizing the "verses of Empedocles" or reciting words before knowing what they mean, or with intellectual pleasure? Just this: it is a pure intellectual pleasure to see precisely why Lucy's response about the sky being "blue" – which it is – is funny. If you don't get it, it "ain't" funny. You don't laugh because you don't see the point. Seeing the point, making proper distinctions, is what philosophy is about, even in comic strips.

Chapter 45

"The Case for Classical Education"

In the *Adoremus Bulletin*, for January 2002, I came across the following letter to the editor: "Can you give me a good response to answer this question which was posed to me by my friend? 'How do I answer my kids when they ask me why we would use a dead language in Mass? They grew up with the Mass in English?'" The editor's response was simply that a) Latin is not a dead language, and b) it is a universal language. Besides that, even "living languages" often become less intelligible because of natural changes – try reading Shakespeare without a dictionary, for example.

Our library has a Chesterton collection. Recently, while browsing there for something on Belloc, I came across Chesterton's essay, "On the Classics," in *Come to Think of It*. Chesterton begins the essay with an account of a young man "in fine frenzy" who maintained in public that "the study of Latin and Greek is not of much use in the battle of life." As an alternative to the study of the "dead languages," the young man proposed that we study something practical, like Health, that is, "the facts and functions of the body." To this Chesterton himself admitted that "I, for one, consistently neglected to do any work at the school in which I was supposed to be learning Latin and Greek...." Chesterton recalls, however, that he did pick up some Latin that came in very handy. He observed that both Samuel Johnson and Robert Louis Stevenson had "this weakness for traditional scholarship," but that neither did "badly in fighting the battle of life."

Chesterton is most amusing and goes to the heart of the matter. "The trouble about always trying to preserve the health of the body is that it is so difficult to do it without destroying the health of the mind. Health is the most unhealthy of all topics." This passage is mindful of a comment in Aristotle in which he remarked that medicine is directed to health as bringing it about, if possible. But when one is healthy, he has no use for a doctor. Health is directed to the things of health, which never are concerned with the body.

Indeed, Chesterton remarks that concern for our health can be quite morbid. There is nothing wrong with knowing what bodily functions are. The young man admitted there is no sense in talking medicine to babies or little children – to which admission Chesterton quips, "every man has a sane spot somewhere." But he thinks that "big boys" should study something practical like health studies. The trouble with the young man is that he does not understand boys. "If you talk to a child about an aortic aneurism, he will not be frightened, he will only be bored. If you talk to a boy of fifteen or sixteen about it, and give only a few fragmentary hints of what it is like, he will very probably come to the rapid conclusion that he has got one." What the boy lacks is that sense of proportion that he would get from a classical education. "Youth is a period when the wildest external carelessness often runs parallel to the most gloomy and concentrated internal cares." I believe it was Chesterton's friend, Shaw, if not Chesterton himself, who said that the only thing that youth lacks is hope, because they do not have enough experience to see alternatives.

So if we revise our school curriculum, which we have indeed, to make our primary study that of the body and not that of the mind, we will put our youth in a most dangerous state. "To throw a medical encyclopedia at the head of a young man in this condition is simply to provide him with a handbook of One Thousand Ways of Going Mad." He will be convinced that he has every disease he reads about. Indeed, Chesterton recalls talking to a professor of medicine who told him that in spite of all the precautions, medical students themselves often suffer from this problem of finding a recently discussed disease in themselves.

What is the issue here? Redolent of the passage in *Orthodoxy* that the madman is the man of one fact, Chesterton points out that advocates of "facts" in education do not really understand what a fact is. "Facts as facts do not always create a spirit of reality, because reality is a spirit. Facts by themselves can often feed a flame of madness, because sanity is a spirit." And this gets to the heart of what Chesterton is driving at. Madmen lack a sense of "proportion in a thing." They really believe that Herodotus wrote Homer, or that the Great Pyramid "was a prophesy of the Great War." Thus, we begin to see that "classical education" is not so "useless in the battle of life." It is not facts that are important but what lies behind and in them, their spirit.

We hear much of the idea of culture. "What culture does, or ought to do, is to give a health of the mind that is parallel to the health of the body. It is ultimately a matter of intellectual instincts. A sane man knows when something would drive him mad, just as a man standing up knows at what angle he would fall down." What causes this sanity is the careful reading of the Latin and Greek works, including the words of Scripture. "That is why the great men I have named, so different in their natures, felt that the classics did count somehow in the battle of life." Practical education is not enough. "Here is the door, here is the open air, *Itur in antiquam silvam.*" We know that for such a mind lunacies will always be lesser matters and sanity be like the open air. The careful reading of the classical authors gives us the image of an ordered soul and ordered city when this ordered life does not exist in the polity or culture to which we belong. This is why it can be said that in the battle of life, the classics free us. This is why we still read them.

Chapter 46

God's Governance

Men are subject to subtle temptations. Perceptive men notice this strange constancy of temptation. The most dangerous of these temptations suggests that, by our own power and ingenuity, we can identify the root problem causing human ills and, by ourselves, eliminate it. At bottom, it is a "technical," not a "personal," problem. We can solve it without solving the question of our souls.

Meanwhile, we are aware that no existing human organization has ever been perfect, however much we would like it to be. Everywhere we look, in time or space, we find the uncanny fact that things continually go wrong. We suspect that they go wrong because of something within each of us. We seek a cause responsible for this deviance. We want to assign blame. We demand accountability.

Of the many memorable lines in Benedict XVI's first encyclical on charity, the following one struck me most: "When we consider the immensity of others' needs, we can… be driven towards an ideology that would aim at doing what God's governance of the world apparently cannot: fully resolving every problem" (#36). Evidently, Christian charity is conceived precisely against this presumption of "resolving every problem." It is a "presumption" because it implies that we can improve on "God's governance of the world," when the Divinity itself failed in this very task.

Among pious, energetic, and liberal people, it is commonplace today to look out on the rest of the world, with all its problems, and earnestly to demand that something be done about it *and soon*. Thinking on a grand scale, we will solve all the problems of every one, especially the poor and weak, if we can just figure out their causes and eliminate them. Perhaps is it the ownership of property? Perhaps it is the family? Perhaps it is the state? All we need do is to identify the problem and eradicate it. A mystical form of secularism seems at work here.

Yet, we now apparently have a pope, no less, warning us precisely against such a facile solution. He even suggests that it is not

Christianity but "ideology" that would aim at this lofty enterprise, as if there is some connection between a wrong solution and a theological proposition.

What is the "theological proposition" at stake? It is that the divine governance is really the root of what is wrong with the human condition. We are ill-made from the beginning. All political ideology thus finds its status as a better proposal, as a cure for something that God could have, but did not, Himself solved. Hence follows the bitter "anti-God" sentiment that is often found in ideology – which means the will to impose our self-generated ideas on the world.

Moreover, the large scope of ideology imitates the even larger scope of the divine governance. Just as Christians are to go forth and baptize *all* nations, so ideology is not content with solving anything less than *all* problems. The ideological solution thus involves the rejection of the *de facto* divine governance as proposed. With this rejection, we need an alternative supplied by the ideology.

The pope is not here suggesting that we should not do what we can about dire human problems, though he understands that they will not completely disappear even with our best efforts. He does not in fact think that government and justice can solve everything. The results of justice are not achieved without charity. That is why this encyclical is a defense of practical charity that itself depends on individual, personal response to real people wherever they are.

Why does the pope find a connection between ideology and the claimed failure of divine governance of the universe? It is because the divine governance includes evil. Or to put it another way, the reason things go wrong is because we have free wills. The location of evil is not in matter, nature, or institutions, but in the power of our wills to choose what is wrong, albeit in the name of choosing something good. Since the ultimate purpose of the divine governance is that we freely choose to love God in the course of our earthly lives, to eliminate this freedom would at the same time eliminate our contact with our highest destiny.

The work of the divine governance is personal. It seeks to save us precisely in our freedom, a freedom that includes our sins as a possibility. The root of ideology is the effort to save us by avoiding any need for us freely to choose the one salvation that is offered to us, the only one that will succeed in the purpose of the divine governance, which is that we may love God and God may love us as persons who also love one another.

Chapter 47

Homo Ambulans

Since the bridge in Minneapolis collapsed not too long ago, the world is bridge-conscious. In natural law class this semester, I said to the class: "What is the 'natural law of bridges?'" I was thinking of J. M. Bochenski's chapter on "law" in his *Philosophy – An Introduction*.

Bochenski shows that a relation exists between mind and the cosmos. A bridge, built by men from antiquity to the present, is designed to provide a way over a river, chasm, or other natural or human obstacle. Bridge builders understand the mathematical and geometric principles enabling them to design precisely a bridge. They know the qualities of stone or other material used in construction.

Thus, bridge builders know the "laws" of the materials they work with, distances, stress, and other elements that go into construction. If they make a mistake in design, the bridge will collapse. Collapsing bridges indicate a correspondence between mind and reality. Our minds know enough about reality to find and use its laws. Once the bridge is built, the "laws" are present in the bridge itself, making it what it is.

Often I walk across the Key Bridge, just below our campus, to the Virginia side across the Potomac. It is a handsome high bridge with several arches. I said to the class, "What does one think before crossing a bridge?" First, he assumes that the "natural law" of bridges is at work within the Key Bridge. Usually we do not think of this, but implicitly assume it. If we did not, we would not put a foot on a bridge.

Secondly, we assume that we are being who can walk. Man is *homo ambulans*. Other animals, of course, walk. Our walking is a function of our definition: *animal rationale*. When we walk across a bridge, we do so for a purpose, not just "to get to the other side." Why do we want to go to the other side? A thousand different reasons, good and bad, exist. We do not always cross for the same reason, but we walk, granted that we could drive, fly, swim, or take a boat if we either wanted to or had to.

Walking across Key Bridge from Virginia, we see the Three Sisters Islands. We note the tide from the Bay, in or out, the trees along the shore, the boat houses. On the rise, we see the Towers of Georgetown. On the opposite side, we see the curve in the river, the Kennedy Center, the Washington Monument, and Roosevelt Island. Overhead are often planes in and out of Reagan Airport. Often below are boats of various types and in the winter ice.

Having some trouble with my leg, it became difficult to walk, a favorite Schall occupation. Suddenly, what it means to be a being that can walk, who has locomotion under the control of his mind and will, takes on a new sense. We did not give ourselves the make-up we have whereby we walk. We find we have it without thinking about it. The world could never work if we did not walk; it is preliminary to almost everything we do.

"So why do we cross a bridge?" Somewhat in the spirit of Hazlett's famous essay "On Going a Journey," we walk because it is itself an exhilarating experience. Yet, the perfection of walking across a bridge is not the fact that we have legs, or that the natural laws of bridges are put there by our minds evidently in conformity with the mind that made things in the first place to be what they are. The natural laws of bridge building were in existence even before there were men who built bridges.

Yet, we walk across the bridges never giving a second thought to the laws of bridges or to the fact that we have legs and can choose what to do with them. If we are not the bridge builders, the bridge is either useful, or beautiful, or pleasant, or sometimes dangerous when its inner laws do not work or our purposes in walking are wrongful. The Last Bridge may also be destroyed in wartime.

Man is *homo ambulans*. This is part of his natural law, the law of reason. This endowment enables him to get to places about his home or to the top of Mt. Rainier, which a student told me he climbed this summer. Walking is a kind of natural reflection of man's mind, which is *capax omnium*, capable of knowing all things. His walking takes him to places he knows. The natural law indicates that relation between all our natural endowments, including our two legs, and our knowing *all that is*. Our walking is a reminder that there really are places and realities outside our minds to which we want to go, at which we want to be present.

Chapter 48

One Man Well Content

One of the books in Everyman's Library is Maisie Ward's 1935 collection of Chesterton's *Stories, Essay's, and Poems.* (*Chesterton's Stories, Essays, and Poem.* Introduction by Maisie Ward (London: Dent, [1957] 1935). In this collection are two poems that strike me as getting to the heart of things, as their titles alone indicate. One is entitled "The Happy Man," the other "The Beatific Vision." We know, of course, that the final end of the happy man, as Aquinas teaches us, is precisely the Beatific Vision by which we see God as He is, as He enables us to see Him in the inner life of the Trinity. The world, I might add, has never much appreciated the path that has led us to this goal, the path of suffering. Indeed, it has hated Him for taking it. One might almost say that much of the history of thought and theology is designed to devise ways of avoiding this glorious truth of our destiny.

"The Beatific Vision" I will take first. It reminds us that the very first step is something that is available to each of us, each day. It begins with a question. The speaker wonders how many "fierce incarnations" he had to pass through before he was "worthy in the world." Worthy of what? Simply worthy "to see a dandelion grow?" We not only see the "one dandelion," the most common of things, but we realize that we are given the power to see it. We realize that we actually see some tiny thing, not only ourselves. We know we see it and are glad.

This is the great act of gratitude at being able to see and be astonished by the most ordinary things, a dandelion growing fixed in the ground. To make this act of gratitude, we must already be outside of ourselves to see the dandelion. We must be sufficiently aware of ourselves to realize that we did not ourselves cause it to be *what it is*, or indeed, to be at all. Thus in a third brief poem, with the Old Testament title "Ecclesiastes," Chesterton begins the same theme of gratitude, now seen from our failure to have it. "There is one sin: to call a green leaf grey...." The sin is to know that the leaf is green, not grey. Things deserve to be called what they are. We do not know what is true unless we affirm of *what is* that it is, unless we say green leaves are green, not grey.

The "naked right to be" happens in the worst of places, in "woes and wars." Yet even there, we do not wish to shame the wrens or show ourselves "unworthy of the grass." A new curiosity occurs. We heard of the "last time when all is told," the judgment of *all that is*. What at that moment shall "God ask of him": who saw what? "He saw her stand beside the hearth, / the firelight garbing her in gold." It is like the seeing of the grass and the wren, so something of a gift. What shall God ask of Him?

Who is this happy man? Whom does he see by the firelight garbed in gold? If we could find this "happy man," we "could bid the heavens repent" of all the anguish of this "grey earth." This is the "gift" we ask. In vain will we search for Him in "feast or mart," nor midst the visions of art. The happy man is grounded in a truth that includes suffering and the disorder of our souls, to which He is called to redeem.

This happy man can only be found in one place, on a "cold hill," on Golgotha. A Trinity is there, "Three persons and one god." This is the ultimate paradox. This is the "happy man." His mother is there. She has seen Him on this earth "beside the hearth."

Why are these short poems of Chesterton so powerful? We surely sense the paradox of the "happy man" and Golgotha. We do not expect to find the Trinity there, though it is in its Word now made flesh, now suffering. The happy man is teaching us that the "Beatific Vision" is in fact why we exist, for what we exist. It is not an abstraction, nor is it offered to us only if we are perfect from our beginnings.

We are men and we sin. Golgotha is not a sign that our finite condition will be perfected in this life. Rather it is a sign that whatever our world is like, best or worst, we are offered the end of the happy man. We must in our lives identify Him, and follow His path, not ours. But creation exists that we achieve the Beatific Vision. Redemption exists that we might achieve it even when by our sins we reject it. But ultimately we must acknowledge in our lives that Golgotha's way is our path, its teaching our lesson, its result is the Resurrection of the flesh. The end of the happy man is the Beatific Vision. The Beatific Vision is the final home of the happy man.

The path to this destiny must be chosen. It begins with gratitude for the lone dandelion, for the fact that it, like ourselves, like the Divinity itself, is rather than is not.

Chapter 49

"The Mystery of Things"

In his discussion about creation, about the things that stand outside of nothingness, things including ourselves, Aquinas, following Genesis, maintains that each existing thing is good. *Omne ens est bonum*. This proposition is a startling affirmation. "How could something be already good if we ourselves did not cause it to be good?" Following Augustine, Aquinas intends to deny the Manichean thesis that material things are created by a god of evil. The origin of evil is not in material things. They are, as such, good. Evil originates in spirit, not matter, in our souls, not our bodies.

We are made, moreover, to know existing things, that they are, that they are good. Our intellects have a certain power of infinity. They are capable of knowing *all that is*. Our minds are not limited "containers" that can only hold so much. They are not "zero-sum" faculties that, in knowing one thing, must give up knowing something else. The most dangerous way to abuse your mind is to refuse to use it. But not just any way of using it will bring you to the truth.

We are not the cause of things. Each thing *that is* has one root in eternity, as it were. We will never come across anything, including ourselves, that we can totally comprehend, even though we are made to comprehend things, whatever they are. The *existence* of anything we know does not fully explain itself. We know that something is, but we do not have the power to make something *to be*. Our proper attitude before anything *that is*, initially, is awe. One end of it always reaches to the source of that strange, exhilarating thing we call *existence*.

Near the end of Shakespeare's *King Lear*, Lear and Cordelia, his beloved daughter, are about to be led off to prison. Cordelia reflects, "We are not the first / Who with best meaning have incurred the worst" (V, iii, 3–18). Lear, Shakespeare's greatest king, has one fault. He loves his youngest daughter wrongly, confusing his role as father with his role as king, both of which are indeed legitimate. Cordelia is "cast down" in thinking of her father's present situation.

But Lear himself refuses to see his imprisonment as a horror if Cordelia is with him. Though many think him mad, he speaks of the glory of things, perhaps itself a form of "madness," as Plato intimated. In prison, Lear and Cordelia shall sing like "birds in a cage." Lear becomes almost lyrical. "When thou dost ask my blessing, I'll kneel down / And pray, and sing, and tell old tales, and laugh / At gilded butterflies, and hear poor rogues / Talk of court news; and we'll talk with them too / Who loses and who wins; who's in, who's out – And take upon's *the mystery of things* / As if we were God's spies...." That is a remarkable, haunting passage. Imagine thinking of ourselves as precisely "God's spies."

Why "God's spies?" Because the reality of all existing things is that behind them lies joy, mirth, and gladness, something we do not see but God does. Lear's "cage" is a place where even pedestrian things become delights.

Lear, next, is asked a blessing. He responds. He will "kneel down." What will he do? He will "pray," and "sing," and yes, tell "old wives tales." But most of all he will laugh at the "gilded butterflies." "Poor rogues" will talk of "court news." And we will not ignore them, these gossipers. We will talk to them too. We have winners and losers, as we know. The implication is that even the losers can win. We are not to despair. Even our faults and sins are capable of being turned around, or perhaps better, following Plato, we can even "turn around" in our sins and faults.

We take upon ourselves "the mystery of things." "What is being taken on?" we wonder. Obviously, the "mystery of things" is already there. Why should we "take it" on ourselves? But what is it that we are to take on? We see that it is this "praying" and "singing" and "telling old wives tales." It is the "laughter" at the gilded butterflies and the court tales of "poor rogues" like ourselves. Lear has caught the wonders of *what is*, not just in its grandeur but in its smallness and ordinariness.

"Is this delight in the presence of ordinary things justified?" It depends upon our theology, our philosophy, on our understanding of *what is*. If we be Manicheans or nihilists or determinists or theoretic voluntarists, it cannot be. Only if the "mystery of things" has its own ground in delight can we suspect that Lear, in his prison, was not mad.

Chapter 50

On Self-Discipline

Everyone has heard that "all work and no play makes Jack a dull boy."
Now, I am not exactly sure just who this famous Jack is, but I suspect
in his own way he is each of us when we confront the notion of precisely *self*-discipline. Clearly, the notion of discipline, especially disciplin-
ing one's own self, has to do with the systematic process by which we
acquire knowledge or virtue or art. Discipline means instruction, especially organized instruction. When we add the notion of "self " to this
instruction, we are indicating that we are ourselves objects of our own
rule, our own need to instruct ourselves. Ultimately, no one else can do
this for us. Our lives are ours to order, to put some sort of principle or
purpose into our many and varied thoughts and deeds. Our lives are
also ours to leave in disorder or in an order that deviates from what it
is we know we ought to be. We should not, moreover, underestimate the
difficulty we confront in ruling ourselves. Christianity even suggests
that most of us might well need something more than ourselves properly to see and rule ourselves.

This topic is really what the First Book of Aristotle's *Ethics* is about
when he tells us reflectively to look back on our deeds and our thoughts
and see, if we can, that for which we act, that which we think to be most
important and that which governs all we do. No doubt we can mislead
ourselves in this self reflection. We can think we act for the noblest purposes, whereas in fact, as all our friends know, we act for money or
pleasure or vain honors. It is difficult to see ourselves as we are, even
if this inner "seeing" is one of the most important things we must do for
ourselves. The famous Socratic admonition, "know thyself," meant at
least this knowledge of our own implicit ends, in addition to knowing
the kind of being we are given by nature – our human being, something
we did not give ourselves.

The student who first comes to the university is no doubt exhila-
rated by a kind of new-found freedom. He is still too young really to
have acquired a good knowledge of himself or a firm capacity to rule

himself. From all I hear, high schools any more are not themselves exactly models of balanced preparations for orderly lives. But I suppose to most high school students in comparison to college, high schools look pretty confined. Many young men and women, no doubt, have, by the time they reach college, already failed to discipline themselves. They have barely begun to acquire the habits and incentives necessary to figure out, not what they should do in terms of a profession or job, but what life itself is about, itself a lifetime task, to be sure. Many of us, unfortunately, make very serious mistakes very early in our lives. College is a place in which, if we are wise, these mistakes can be either corrected or, on the contrary, magnified infinitely.

Now, I am not someone who thinks that we will really learn what life itself is about in college courses. We may, no doubt, get snippets here and there. The ideology or intellectual chaos that is often, as many critics point out, the meaning of college curricula themselves needs to be reflected on and understood. Universities and colleges are there to be "used." We are not to attend them blindly, even though we can and must make ourselves teachable. A good number of the very important books and ideas that a student will need to know if he is to know the truth, to confront what is good, are never even mentioned in any university curriculum or course. This situation would imply that we need to know something about life even before beginning to learn more specifically about parts of it in an academic setting. If we are lucky, we begin to suspect that some of these things we need to know, the highest things, come from our parents or our church or our friends or our own curiosity. Many a man has saved his soul because of some book he chanced to read in some obscure library or used book store. Many a girl has understood what her life is about because she happened, one random summer afternoon, to talk seriously to her grandmother or to her aunt.

Self-discipline, the rule over all of our given passions, fears, dreams, thoughts, can be, if simply taken for itself, a dangerous thing. We can be Stoics who conceive self-discipline somehow as an end in itself, whereas it is really the prerequisite for seeing and loving what is not ourselves. Self-discipline can become a form of pride in which we attribute to ourselves complete mastery over ourselves with no willingness to guide ourselves to ends that are to be served or people to be loved. None the less, our "bare" selves are objects to ourselves. We recognize that our ability to accomplish anything at all begins with some realization that we must take control of ourselves. We must begin to note in ourselves those things that cause us troubles. Plato said that the worst thing that can happen to us is to have a lie in our souls, especially about ourselves. These difficulties can even be other students, perhaps even teachers, who interfere with our studies or our responsibilities, including our responsibilities to God. They can be things like drink or drugs or our own laziness.

The purpose of self-discipline in the best sense then is not ourselves. That probably sounds strange. The classical writers, I think, used to relate self-discipline to liberty. The person who was most free was the one who had the most control over himself. The person who was most un-free was the one who was ruled by pleasures, money, or power. Self-discipline does not, however, solve the question of what is knowledge or truth or good. In this sense, it is instrumental, something good for the sake of something else. John Paul II put it well in his profound new book, "the fundamental dimension of man's existence… is always a co-existence."

We are ourselves to be sure and we are to rule ourselves. But once we have managed to approach this no doubt difficult issue, what remains is the rest of our lives. We can then begin to focus on the things of the highest importance and dignity, something we would be unable to do if we did not succeed in imposing some self-discipline on ourselves. Paul Johnson in his book, *The Intellectuals*, has suggested, with considerable unpopularity, that there is an intimate connection between our moral life and our intellectual life. Sometimes, I think the history of our times can be described as an argument on whether or not this connection is true. Self-discipline is the beginning of wisdom, not its end. When we have discovered the purpose for which self-discipline exists, we will, if we are sane, hardly recall anything about it because it has enabled us to become free to see so much else.

Chapter 51

On Hazlitt's "Going"

Several yeas ago, I had a student by the name of Joe Flahive. For such a young man, he was an amazing linguist, knew the classical tongues, knew theology, philosophy. I suspect his teachers were somewhat afraid of him. He told me he played baseball in high school in Connecticut, and he could play the piano. He told me that his grandmother played ragtime piano some place, but he also knew classical piano. As I had never heard the music that is in Belloc's *A Path to Rome* played or sung before, I asked him one afternoon if he would mind playing it and singing it for me. He was delighted to do so. We have a piano in one of our parlors where he finally let Schall hear what Belloc sang.

This young man one summer joined a program in Rome with the Pope's Latinist. I believe they were dealing with *Veritatis Splendor.* After a summer in Latin studies at the Vatican, I recall, he flew to Inverness in Scotland. From there, having somehow secured boots, he proceeded to walk to the North Sea and back to Inverness before he returned to the States. He evidently stayed in inns or slept out of doors, ate from local fare. I forget now how long it took him, maybe twelve days. He walked by himself.

One of the most famous, if not the most famous English walking essay is that of William Hazlitt, "On Going a Journey," published in *The New Monthly Magazine,* January, 1822. Hazlitt (1780–1830) was the son of a Unitarian minister. After a try, he did not follow his father's profession but became basically a journalist and writer.

Today, one hesitates to think there are those who have not read this most charming essay. Indeed, on rereading it, it is so familiar that one is tempted to think it full of cliches, so much of what Hazlitt wrote has become part of the language and the sentiment of walking. The very first thing that one notices about the essay is that the title lacks a preposition. The title is not "On Going *on* a Journey," but simply "On Going a Journey." I hesitate making a big issue of this terminology, but somehow the lack of the preposition makes the mood of the essay more immediate, more personal.

Hazlitt distinguishes between walking in one's native places and walking in foreign lands. For the first we do not want anyone else but ourselves. For the latter we need a companion. Hazlitt does not mention political conditions – that is, not every polity welcomes our walking around by ourselves. Robbery of hapless walkers is not unknown in this century, or any century. There are some places, however, where the walker is still welcome. I write these lines conscious that Belloc's *The Path to Rome* was set in the year 1901, while his *Four Men* in 1902, both magnificent walking books.

Hazlitt, moreover, does not, besides politics, mention dogs! I presume he had a sturdy stick and was capable of wielding it, if necessary. I have always found that the most uncomfortable part of any countryside, or city-side for that matter, walk, even in friendly climes, was the furiously barking dog racing to catch my fleeing heels. I have never met the owner of a vicious dog who admitted that it would bite. This experience has always served to undermine any confidence in the observational powers of dog-owners. Basically, do not believe them, or, if you do, keep yourself well supplied with rabies injections.

The main part of Hazlitt's essay is really devoted to teaching us a kind of active contemplation. "I can enjoy society in a room," Hazlitt tells us, "but out of doors, nature is company enough for me. I am never less alone than when I am alone." Hazlitt does not put this last sentence in quotation marks. But at the beginning of Part III of Cicero's *De Officiis*, we read: "Publius Cornelius Scipio, the first of that family to be called Africanus, used to remark that he was never less idle than when he had nothing to do, and never less lonely than when he was by himself." The sentiment stands at the core of our personal existence

"The soul of a journey is liberty," Hazlitt continues, "perfect liberty, to think, feel, do just as one pleases." Presumably, Hazlitt does not mean here a Machiavellian liberty, the exhilarating freedom to do wrong if it aids one's success. We have the impression that the man is getting out of his routine, taking a look at things he has never seen before, though there is nothing wrong with seeing, on our walks, the same things again and again.

Yet, Hazlitt recognizes that the walker must dine. In fact, the more he walks, the more the anticipation of food at the end of the day entices him. "I grant there is one subject on which it is pleasant to talk on a journey, and that is, what one shall eat for supper when we get to our inn at night." Hazlitt has a place for what he calls, evidently following Luther, "Table-Talk." But that is reserved for indoors. How charming is Hazlitt! "How fine it is to enter some old town, walled and turreted, just at approach of nightfall, or to come to some straggling village, with the lights streaming through the surrounding gloom; and then, after inquiring for the best entertainment that the place affords, to 'take one's ease at one's inn.'!"

I had noted that the phrase "take one's ease at one's inn" was in quotation marks. It is given in the *Oxford Dictionary of Quotations* as from *Henry IV*, P. I, iii. iii, 91 (77). How remarkable it is that the English language can so associate a man walking by himself with the coming to an inn that recalls Falstaff and Henry, though I should add that in this inn, Falstaff is complaining about getting his pocket picked!

Hazlitt is content to pass time in the inn. "It was on the 10th of April, 1798, that I sat down to a volume of the *New Eloise*, at the inn at Llangollen, over a bottle of sherry and a cold chicken." Somehow, I confess a less than gluttonous desire for such a dietary combination at any inn. But a man reveals himself more by what he reads, when he is free, than by what he eats after a long day's walk, though he reveals himself in both.

"We change our place, we change our ideas; nay, our opinions and feelings." It is indeed difficult, I think, to be in a foreign land. We measure the universe by ourselves, and even comprehend the texture of our own being only piecemeal." Hazlitt relented somewhat on his strictures about foreign travel when he went to Calais in France. He did think we are somehow different people outside our own lands. Ultimately, he tries to have the best of both worlds: "We can be said only to fill our destiny in the place that gave us birth. I should on this account like well enough to spend the whole of my life in travelling abroad, if I could anywhere borrow another life to spend afterwards at home."

Somehow this passage makes me think of Cobbett's *Rural Rides*, a book, as I recall, full of accounts of people who never get but a few miles from their place of birth. Hazlitt actually cites Cobbett: "He thought it a bad French custom to drink our wine with our meals, and that an Englishman ought to do only one thing at a time." I was born on a farm near Pocahontas, Iowa. Almost all the barns, sheds, houses, and outbuildings that I recall from youth are now destroyed; the plots are now all farm land. As far as I know, few walk there, though all states have walking trails. What indeed is "our destiny in the place that gave us birth?"

Chapter 52

What Philosophers Play With

In the *Notebooks* (*Carnet de Notes*) of the French philosopher Jacques Maritain, I came across this amusing entry from April 10, 1906: "Philosophers play with fire (poets also). Nothing is as comical as a course at the Sorbonne, in which an enervated professor expounds his historical views to some dunces, and discusses David Hume as peacefully as Plato. Does this seem dead to you? Fortunately, not the slightest spark flies!" The reader can relax. Schall, enervated or otherwise, is not about to expound on David Hume, except for one shinning moment.

That moment came years ago while reading Charles N. R. McCoy's much neglected book, *The Structure of Political Thought*. In discussing what he called "The Outcome of Autonomous Natural Law," McCoy came to Hume. "Since the intention of this teaching was to show the absence of any necessity in nature, it followed also that – as Hume expressly stated it – 'the contrary of every matter of fact is… possible, because it can never imply a contradiction, and is conceived by the mind with the same facility and distinctness as if ever so conformable to reality'" (226). This passage provided for me a most luminous moment of understanding.

For the logic of Hume explained how a philosophy could make the very world in front of him disappear. If the principle of contradiction did not hold, if anything that stood before me could be the opposite of what it was, we have already here the intelligibility of all forms of voluntarism be it in theology, in science, or in politics. The principle had antecedents found in the *Euthyphro*, in Duns Scotus, in Islam. The will God, the Prince, or the Philosopher could make everything disappear.

Modern philosophy was left with the task of having to explain how the world could exist when it had just proved that what was before its very face could, while still there, be its opposite. What was left was only its own imaginings fortified by science and technology. The real task in the modern world, however, as I later learned from Chesterton, is to restore reason to be reason, something that only faith seemed interested in doing. The tepid "spark" of Hume's principle, as it were, was that of a dying actual world. I found it, I must confess, eye-opening.

Plato, however, is another matter. It is, I have found, difficult to read Plato without sparks or fire. Of course, anyone who knows Plato, especially the *Laws*, is familiar with the special use that the verb "to play" has in his philosophy. We would likely read Maritain's good phrase – "Philosophers play with fire" – to mean that its subject matter is a dangerous, burning thing, to be approached with the greatest caution, like firemen going to confront a furious blaze. But then firemen are not described as "playing" in a frolicking water fight before the flames.

The notion that philosophy could be thought to be dull or useless also goes back to Plato. So does the notion that it is not, that it is fire. Socrates spent his time roaming Athens, as he tells us, as a "gadfly," as someone who wanted to wake the citizens up to examine their lives about the important things This awakening was something they were so reluctant to do. They figured it was easier to get rid of Socrates rather than follow his proddings. So they eliminated him in an act that, perhaps more than any other, has kept philosophy alive among us. Philosophy has a bad name whenever and wherever it has ceased to be what it is, a pursuit of the truth.

When Socrates turned his attention to our lives, he said that they were not important. He was not being funny, but he was being paradoxical. He did not mean that we did not need food, clothing, shelter, even perhaps some luxuries, as Glaucon rather contemptuously described the situation in the *Republic*. It is not that there was nothing serious in the universe. The trick was to find what it was. This "finding" was what philosophy was about. We are thus called the "playthings" of the gods. Socrates tells us that this status is the best thing about us. We cannot help but be astonished at this news about which probably no one has ever told us.

Philosophy is a quest for the whole. It is fire. It is interesting that the Scriptural images of Hell are also often those of fire, as if to say that our pursuit of the truth is not an indifferent process. Rather it is something so important that the fear of burning is what incites us to pursue it, lest we fail to achieve what we are. The "contrary of every matter of fact is possible." If it is, we are not. It is against this conclusion that the gates of Hell and the fields of play before the Lord are set up to assure us, in spite of our philosophy to the contrary, that we really exist.

Philosophers and poets play with fire. When we were young, our parents warned us not to play with fire. After we are adults, philosophers turn around and tell us to play with it at the cost of our very being. The fire that we play with is the daily examination of what we are. Fire is light. We search for light, for knowing *what is* in its lightness, in its source. The contrary of every matter of fact is not possible. *What is* is.

The playthings of the gods, that is, we ourselves, need not have existed. The gods do not "need" us. In the end, the source of our greatness is that we are, but need not be. The philosophical quest for the whole discovers that we are not the whole, but our very wanting to know it takes us to that final thing in the universe that Socrates said is "serious." Maritain was right. We should not waste out time with dull professors if they do not tell us this.

Chapter 53

On "Everlasting Futurity"

One of my Jesuit colleagues, Alvaro Ribiero, called my attention to the last entry, No. 103, in Samuel Johnson's series in *The Idler*. The date was Saturday, 5 April 1760. After he recited by heart the last lines of this magnificent essay, I hastened to find my copy of Johnson to read it again, and again. It is a haunting essay. Nothing less can be said about it than it is the *best* of things to be read, preferably out loud, about the *last* of things.

No better introduction to a column series entitled "Last Things," in an on–line journal unabashedly entitled, *First Principles*, could be imagined. Only one without a soul, and there may be not a few, would not know the origin of these phrases about first and last things. For they recall the Alpha and the Omega, the beginning and the end, starting and ending points of our very being, of *what is*. I believe there are lines in T. S. Eliot, in "Ash Wednesday," that read "in the end is my beginning." *Prima Principia. Ultimus Finis.*

Technically, a "first principle" is a beginning point of thought, that behind which there is no behind except being itself. A first principle is that which cannot be "proved" because nothing clearer can be found than the statement itself. Likewise, there are first principles of being, of *what is*. To deny a first principle, you have to use it in the denial. This means that the mind itself works in a certain way that is itself simply there, simply given, simply true. The person with a mind does not make mind to be mind. He discovers that he himself has mind by reflecting on himself knowing what is not himself. He knows that he is doing so. He tries to express the truth of things by himself affirming what he knows.

The last *Idler* was published during Holy Week, a time, as Johnson remarks, "set apart for the examination of the conscience." This time allows us to "review" life. Johnson is conscious of his readers. He wants them to "review every incident (of life) with seriousness and improve it by meditation." How might we "improve" ourselves by "meditation" on such serious moments? By the very fact that we see within them the sign of our freedom, that what is there in our acts we put there by our choice. Know thyself.

The moments of our lives are not only "lived" but also remembered. Thus, they can be "reviewed" by us. Our memory gives us the strange power of seeing our actions again. In this sense, we can live more than once. What we can remember, others can know. We can seek to repair our past when we know in our memory how we contributed to it. And we can rejoice that at least some of our deeds are noble. This reminds us of Augustine. We are not only what we are, but we are what we remember. A man without memory, who is mindful of nothing, cannot see what he is. The man with a memory can see himself again. Of human living, once is never enough.

Johnson humbly asks his readers to reflect that the series of "trifles" that he has written over the years are being "brought to a conclusion." Indeed, the readers will themselves outlive the existence of the journal once it ceases. "An end must in time be put to everything great as to everything little." What a wonderful sentence! Time and all things are related in their end. One recalls now those two-and-more-centuries-old gentlemen who first read the last *Idler* and outlived it. We are the ones who now read it, not they. And the same fate will be ours. *Scripta manet.*

"To life must come its last hour, and to this system of being its last day." Meditation on the last things is essential to our being what we are. Socrates faced his last hour calmly, because he knew death was not the greatest evil. Johnson is a Christian though in no way a doubter of Socratic wisdom here. There will be an "hour at which probation ceases, and repentance will be vain." Life is also a "probation." There is a time for repentance. We have been "tested." We can make up for our sins by repentance. We are given time to define what we are, what we profess to be when we "cease."

Still, a day comes "in which every work of the hand and imagination of the heart shall be brought to judgment." Benedict XVI's encyclical *Spe Salvi* is precisely written about this very topic of judgment that Johnson knew so well. To judge means to state the truth of what we make ourselves to be in our words and deeds. The world cannot exist, cannot be complete, without "judgment." Plato already understood this in the last book of the *Republic*. An un-judged world is an unjust world. Of such is why both immortality and resurrections are questions of justice and judgment. Benedict says he learned this from the Marxist philosopher Theodor Adorno who believed in neither immortality nor resurrection.

What follows from this "judgment?" Johnson's words are precise, "an *everlasting futurity* shall be determined by the past." This determination of our "futurity" is thus in our hands. Our past is only determined because it was free. But the judgment cannot be ours alone, lest we recreate the world in our image and thereby miss the very *futurity* that awaits us.

First principles lead to the last things. As Johnson poignantly said earlier in the same essay, "We seldom learn the true want of what we have till it is discovered that we can have it no more." Notice that Johnson speaks of "the true want of what we have." Thus the question is not, "Do we have it?" but, "Do we know what we have and are and, knowing it, yes, remember it?"

This last essay of *The Idler* begins, as many of these essays do, with a Greek or Latin citation setting the theme of what Johnson is to write about. For the last essay, Johnson chose a passage from Juvenal's Tenth Satire, which Johnson himself translated as "The Vanity of Human Wishes." The passage reads: "*Respicere ad longae jussit spatia ultima vitae.*" Evidently this is from a conversation between Solon, the wise lawgiver, and Croesus, the rich man. Taking his image from a chariot race, Solon tells him to look to the last lap (*spatium*) or round of a long life. Long lives have a last lap. First principles. Last end. The Alpha and the Omega.

Conclusion

None of the books of collected essays in my possession has a conclusion. And there is probably no excuse for a conclusion to this selection. Still, I want to add some words to what is gathered here. At the very beginning of this book are found six citations that were put there because they seemed to me to preview the ideas that are found in *The Classical Moment*. One of these passages was from Aristotle, one from Samuel Johnson, one from a Psalm, one from Shakespeare, one from Plato, and one from Belloc.

The first citation was from Aristotle. It simply tells us that we know things when we know the reason for them, when we know that a "fact could not be other than it is." Johnson warns us about reading well when we are young. We are to "read hard," as he put it. Our judgments may improve but our "poring upon books" when we are older may prove to be an "irksome task." The Psalm speaks of gladness, of the House of the Lord. It hints, as does life itself, that we have here no lasting city.

King Lear brings us to the "mystery of things," which we are to "take upon's." We need forgiveness, yes, to tell "old tales," to pray, to "sing and to laugh." Plato tells us that we are not here simply to survive and to exist with no inner knowings or pleasures. We are to seek virtue "as long as life lasts." And finally there is Belloc's recalling that "hunger for home," that pervades all that we seek or read or write or remember. It is as the Psalmist had said.

On Candlemas Day, 2007, I received a book from a former student who was studying in Toronto. The title of the book was *A Book of English Essays (1600–1900)*. It was first published in 1912. The reprint is dated 1914, the beginning of the Great War. It was published by Oxford University Press in The World's Classics Series.

The book contains 52 essays, not 53 as does this book. In this "no conclusion" collection, we find an essay of George Elliot entitled, "Authorship." In it she writes: "It is for art to present images of a lovelier order than the actual, gently winning the affections and so determining the taste." This sentiment is true, I think, provided that it does not prevent us from the more important adventure of seeing the loveliness of what is about us, of *what is*. It has been the purpose of this collection to see that too.

This book bears a dedication from Nicholas Wheeler, the young man who sent it to me. It reads:

> I acquired this little collection of essays two years ago when I was in Oxford, and should like you to have it. I especially appreciate Sir Thomas Browne's essay "On Dreams" – "That some have never dreamed, is as improbable as that some have never laughed"; Dr. Johnson's "On the Advantages of Living in a Garrett" – "I never think myself qualified to judge a man whom I have only known in one degree of elevation"; and Matthew Arnold on "Dante and Beatrice" – "Dante saw the world, and used in his poetry what he had seen; for he was a born artist. But he was essentially aloof from the world, and not complete in the life of the world; for he was a born spiritualist and solitary."

I was touched by the expression, "I should like you to have it." This is the gift theme that has often come up in these pages. Here we have these themes again, the dreams, the laughter; we have Beatrice and what we see when we are alone.

As I mentioned in the beginning, Belloc has an essay "On Everything." In this book, Henry Fielding has "An Essay on Nothing." I believe between the two, we might find everything about which we might write essays. In Leigh Hunt's essay on Shakespeare, he says of the Bard that "Whether grieving us or making us glad, thou makest us kinder and happier." Finally, Jonathan Swift writes: "For nature has left every man a capacity, though not of shining in company; and there are a hundred men sufficiently qualified for both, who, by a very few faults, that they might correct in half an hour, are not so much as tolerable." Between our faults and our virtues stand our wills and our habits.

So virtue and vice, everything and nothing are what we have read about here. The man who never dreams is as unlikely as the man who never laughs. Dante saw the particular world because he was first a solitary, something that Cicero had also remarked when he said that he was "never less alone than when he was by himself."

We must first be moved. There are moments in our lives, yes, "classical moments," when we are simply struck by what we see or hear, by whom we meet, by how things are. It is from these moments that our real lives begin and flourish, however long we have already been living.